· SPOTLIGHT · ON LITERACY

Authors, Consultants, and Reviewers

MULTICULTURAL AND EDUCATIONAL
CONSULTANTS

Alma Flor Ada, Yvonne Beamer, Joyce Buckner,
Helen Gillotte, Cheryl Hudson, Narcita Medina,
Lorraine Monroe, James R. Murphy, Sylvia Peña,
Joseph B. Rubin, Ramon Santiago, Cliff Trafzer,
Hai Tran, Esther Lee Yao

LITERATURE CONSULTANTS

Ashley Bryan, Joan I. Glazer, Paul Janeczko,
Margaret H. Lippert

INTERNATIONAL CONSULTANTS

Edward B. Adams, Barbara Johnson,
Raymond L. Marshall

MUSIC AND AUDIO CONSULTANTS

John Farrell, Marilyn C. Davidson,
Vincent Lawrence, Sarah Pirtle, Susan R. Synder,
Rick and Deborah Witkowski, Eastern Sky Media
Services, Inc.

TEACHER REVIEWERS

Terry Baker, Jane Bauer, James Bedi, Nora Bickel,
Vernell Bowen, Donald Cason, Jean Chaney,
Carolyn Clark, Alan Cox, Kathryn DesCarpentrie,
Carol L. Ellis, Roberta Gale, Brenda Huffman,
Erma Inscore, Sharon Kidwell, Elizabeth Love,
Isabel Marcus, Elaine McCraney, Michelle Moraros,
Earlene Parr, Dr. Richard Potts, Jeanette Pulliam,
Michael Rubin, Henrietta Sakamaki,
Kathleen Cultron Sanders, Belinda Snow,
Dr. Jayne Steubing, Margaret Mary Sulentic,
Barbara Tate, Seretta Vincent,
Willard Waite, Barbara Wilson, Veronica York

Macmillan/McGraw-Hill

A Division of The McGraw-Hill Companies

Copyright © 2000, 1999 McGraw-Hill School Division,
a Division of the Educational and Professional
Publishing Group of The McGraw-Hill Companies, Inc.

McGraw-Hill School Division
Two Penn Plaza
New York, New York 10121
Printed in the United States of America

ISBN 0-02-185879-9 / 2, L. 7

3 4 5 6 7 8 9 071 03 02 01 00

Spotlight on Literacy

AUTHORS

ELAINE MEI AOKI • VIRGINIA ARNOLD • JAMES FLOOD • JAMES V. HOFFMAN • DIANE LAPP

MIRIAM MARTINEZ • ANNEMARIE SULLIVAN PALINCSAR • MICHAEL PRIESTLEY • CARL B. SMITH

WILLIAM H. TEALE • JOSEFINA VILLAMIL TINAJERO • ARNOLD W. WEBB • KAREN D. WOOD

 **Macmillan McGraw-Hill**

NEW YORK • FARMINGTON

Unit 1

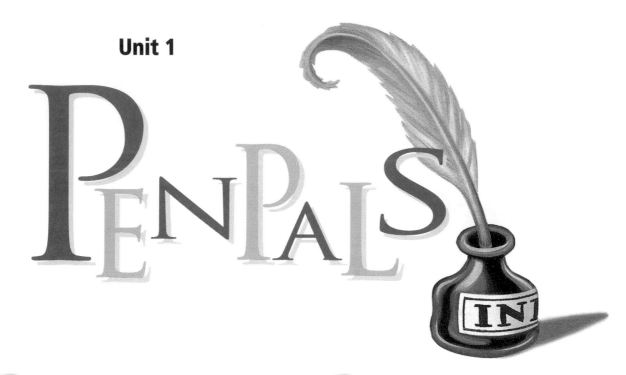

PENPALS

Unit 2

HAND in HAND

6

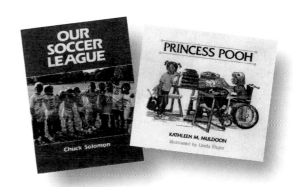

7

Unit 3

NATURE'S WAY

8

9

Unit 1

PenPals

When Philippe Dupasquier moved from France to London, England, he thought about his family in France and wondered what they were doing. *"Dear Daddy . . .* came from that," he says. "If you're away from someone you care about, thinking of what they are doing makes you feel less alone."

Mr. Dupasquier lives in the countryside near London. He says, "You are isolated here, so small things that happen are important. You notice the little things like cars in the streets and the changing of the seasons. I watched things around me and put them into *Dear Daddy . . .* Most of the ideas for the book came from things that happened in my family and from things I saw around me in England."

Air Mail

Mr. John Slater
S.S. Eternity
Jefferson Lines
c/o Frederick Morse Agt.
Hong Kong

Meet
Philippe Dupasquier

Dear Daddy...

PHILIPPE DUPASQUIER

Dear Daddy,
I think about you lots and lots. Are you all right on your
ship? We all miss you.

It's raining all the time at home, so Mommy bought me
some red boots. They're great!

Mr. Green the gardener came to trim the hedge today.
Timmy's got a new tooth. He's got six altogether now.

Mommy says he'll soon be walking. I hope you are well.
We think about you all the time.

I had a great birthday party. All my friends came, except for Jacky—she had chicken-pox. Mommy made a chocolate cake.

I had lots and lots of presents. My best one was a mask for looking underwater when we go to the beach.

School has started again. The garden is full of dead leaves.
The teacher showed me on a big map where you are
going on your ship.

She said it was a very long way. I wish you were
home again.

It's very cold and Timmy is sick. Dr. Rush came and he
looked in Timmy's mouth and listened to his chest with
a stethoscope. He said it's not too bad, and Mommy
went to buy some medicine.

I liked the postcard you sent us. There's lots of snow here. Timmy and me made a huge snowman. Mommy says if I'm good, Santa Claus might bring me a bicycle. That would be great!

23

Some men from the music shop brought back the old piano today. They have fixed it. Mommy is very happy.

She's going to teach me how to play it. Then when I'm big, I'll be a pianist and go around the world just like you.

When you come home, we'll do all sorts of things together.
We can go walking in the woods, and fishing in the pond,
just like we used to . . .

and at night-time, we'll look up at the sky and you can
tell me the story of the little prince who lives on a star.

It's not long till summer and I know we'll soon be all together again.

I think about you every day. Please come home quickly.

Love from Sophie

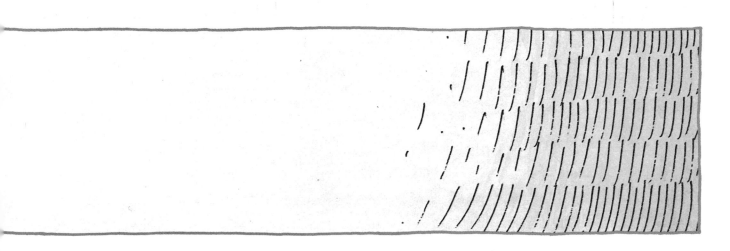

Postcards from the Earth

Here are some postcards from different parts of the world. These places hold weather records.

So grab an umbrella, put on your swimsuit, don't forget your coat and hang on to your hat ... here we go!

Desert of Atacama

This desert is in the longest, narrowest country in the world. Chile is 2,650 miles long. The Desert of Atacama is one of the driest places on earth. It rains here only a couple of times every decade!

Winds at Commonwealth Bay, Antarctica, are as strong as a hurricane. The winds can blow as fast as 200 miles an hour. Commonwealth Bay is one of the windiest places on earth.

Commonwealth Bay, Antarctica

Vostok, Antarctica

You better dress in lots of layers if you're going to visit Vostok, near the South Pole. It is one of the coldest places on earth. It's not unusual to have temperatures as cold as -128 degrees Fahrenheit here. That's 160 degrees below freezing!

Every year about 460 inches of rain falls on Mount Waialeale, Hawaii. It is the wettest place in the world.

Mt. Waialeale, Hawaii

San Luis, Mexico

The hottest recorded temperature on Earth was in San Luis, Mexico. It got as hot as 136 degrees Fahrenheit. That's only 76 degrees from the boiling point!

Eletelephony

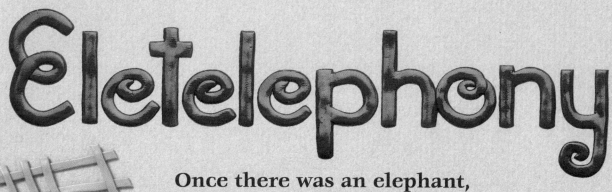

Once there was an elephant,
Who tried to use the telephant—
No! no! I mean an elephone
Who tried to use the telephone—
(Dear me! I am not certain quite
That even now I've got it right.)

Howe'er it was, he got his trunk
Entangled in the telephunk;
The more he tried to get it free,
The louder buzzed the telephee—
(I fear I'd better drop the song
Of elephop and telephong!)

Laura E. Richards

Write about a radish
Too many people write about the moon.

The night is black
The stars are small and high
The clock unwinds its ever-ticking tune
Hills gleam dimly
Distant nighthawks cry.
A radish rises in the waiting sky.

Karla Kuskin

✳ Meet James Stevenson

James Stevenson began writing and drawing as a child. He loved to watch movies and read comic books. He says that both activities influenced the books he writes for children.

He says, "I think that my experience and creative mind have been formed by movies and comic books. I like to write. I like to draw. I like to paint. And in writing picture books I found a way to tell a story without using just words."

When asked if he prefers drawing to writing, he said, "I think that drawing is the more childlike and natural. When you're a little kid, you grab crayons, you don't grab the typewriter. I think drawing is a little more fun than writing, but whether it's more satisfying by the time you're old, I don't know."

BEST WISHES, ED

by JAMES STEVENSON

Ed lived on a big island of ice
with Betty, Freddy, Al,
and a lot of other penguins.
Every day they had fun
throwing snowballs
and sliding on the ice.

But they always watched out
for Ernest, the big whale.
Every time he went by . . .
SPLAT!
Ed and everybody got soaked.

"Watch what you are doing!"
Betty would yell.

But Ernest swam right by.
"Ernest doesn't even notice penguins,"
said Ed.

One night when Ed was asleep,
there was a loud cracking noise.
It sounded like ice breaking.
Ed thought it was a dream.

When Ed woke up in the morning,
he found that the island of ice
had broken in half.
He was all alone
on an island of his own.

Ed's friends got smaller
and smaller
as his island drifted away.
Ed watched until he couldn't
see them anymore.

Then he walked
around his island.
There was nobody on it at all.
At last he came to his
own footprints again.

Some birds flew over.
Ed waved,
but they did not wave back.
"I guess I will be here
the rest of my life," Ed said.
At the end of the day,
he wrote "I GIVE UP"
in big letters in the snow.
Then he went to sleep.

In the morning a tern woke him up.
"Hey," said the tern,
"did you write that thing in the snow?"

"Yes," said Ed.

"Could you write something
for me?" asked the tern.

"I guess so," said Ed.
"What do you want?"

49

"Tell my friends to meet me
at the blue iceberg," said the tern.
"And sign it 'Talbot.'
That is my name."

Talbot flew away,
and Ed wrote the message.

MEET
TALBOT
AT THE
BLUE
ICEBERG

Pretty soon, Talbot's friends
flew over and read the message.
They waved to Ed,
and Ed waved back.

HAROLD:
YOUR SUPPER IS READY

All day long, birds stopped and asked Ed
to write messages for them.
By the end of the day, the whole island
was covered with messages.
Ed was very tired.

DOROTHY:
MARTHA IS
LOOKING FOR YOU

GEORGE
MARY
IS AT

Talbot landed and gave Ed a fish.
"You are doing a great job,"
said Talbot.
"How come you look so gloomy?"

"I miss my friends
on my old island," said Ed.

"Where is your old island?"
asked Talbot.

"Way over there someplace,"
said Ed.

"Too bad you can't fly," said Talbot.
"You could spot it from the air."

"Well, I can't fly," said Ed.

"It's not very hard," said Talbot.

"It is for penguins," said Ed.

Talbot flew away.
"I guess I will spend the rest
of my life writing messages,"
Ed said to himself.

When Ed got up the next morning,
he found a surprise.

ED — THERE'S
A MESSAGE
FOR YOU!

FOLLOW THE ARROWS

He followed the arrows
until he came to another message.

He sat down on the X
and waited.

Suddenly there was a great SPLAT!
Ed was soaked.
It was Ernest.
"I understand you are looking
for a ride to that island
with all the penguins on it,"
said Ernest.

"How did you know?" asked Ed.

"Talbot told me," said Ernest.
"Hop aboard."

"Wait one second," said Ed.
"I have to leave a message."

"Well, make it snappy," said Ernest.
"I have other things to do
besides give rides to penguins."

Ed quickly wrote
the message in the snow.

THANK YOU,
TALBOT.
BEST WISHES,
Ed

Then he climbed
on top of Ernest's back.
Ernest gave a couple of
big splashes with his tail,
and then they were racing
across the water.

"Ed is back!" yelled Betty.

"Hooray!" shouted Freddy and Al.

Ed slid off Ernest's back.
"Thanks a lot, Ernest," called Ed.

"That's O.K.," said Ernest.
"Just don't expect a ride every day."

"We're so glad you are back, Ed,"
said Betty.

"We missed you a lot,"
said Freddy and Al.

"I missed you," said Ed.

SPLAT! They were all soaked,
as Ernest swam away.

"Hey," said Betty, "he did it again!"

"Ernest doesn't notice penguins,"
said Freddy.

"Sometimes he does," said Ed.

There was an
~ old pig ~
with a pen

There was an old pig with a pen
Who wrote stories and verse now and then.
To enhance these creations,
He drew illustrations
With brushes, some paints and his pen.

There was an old pig with a pen
Who had finished his work once again.
Then he quietly sat
With his comfortable cat . . .

While he rested his brushes and pen.

Arnold Lobel

And Then

I was reading
a poem
about snow

when
the sun
came out
and
melted it.

Prince Redcloud

PUFF...
FLASH...
BANG!

A BOOK ABOUT SIGNALS
by Gail Gibbons

The traffic light turns red. A church bell bongs.
The police-car siren screams. A football referee throws
both arms above his head. All of these are signals.

People use signals to say things to each other without using spoken or written words. We see or hear most signals.

Thousands of years ago . . .

Ancient Romans set fires on mountaintops or on hills to send different messages over long distances. These fires are called beacon fires. One beacon fire signals to ships that there are dangerous cliffs nearby.

On the flatlands, a fire warns waiting troops that the enemy is fast approaching.

Later in time, and in another part of the world, people use drums to send messages. A tribesman beats out a signal to nearby villages saying there is to be a great feast.

Horns are used to make signals, too. On a Viking ship a horn blasts its warning to soldiers on shore. A raiding party is coming!

Across the ocean . . .

A Native American quickly pulls a blanket off a damp, smoking fire. A puff of smoke rises up toward the sky, telling people that the harvest is about to begin. The number of puffs changes depending on the signal.

Other Native Americans use columns of smoke for signals. One column of smoke means "Pay attention!" Two columns of smoke mean "All is well." Three columns of smoke . . . "Danger!"

During the American Revolution, soldiers use cannon as signals. The cannon are spaced miles apart. The first one is fired. Its sound travels to the next group of soldiers. They fire their cannon. Then a third burst sounds. And a fourth cannon fires. This is a loud relay of cannon bursts signaling that all troops must advance.

Meanwhile, Paul Revere plans a signal to warn
the people of Boston that British troops are going to
attack. He waits on horseback while a friend watches
from a tall church belfry. Lanterns will be the signal.
One lantern means the British are coming by land . . .
two lanterns, by sea. Two lanterns shine! Paul Revere
makes his famous ride, shouting the warning.

Today, many signals are sight signals.

Lights are signals we see every day. Some cars stop at the intersection and others go. A traffic light tells the drivers what they should do.

Cars have light signals, too. They have turn signals, brake signals, and bright and dim headlights for other cars and trucks to see.

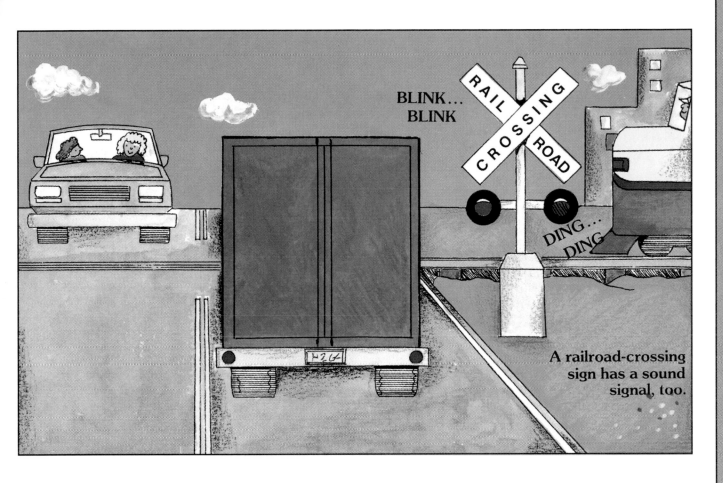

A railroad-crossing
sign has a sound
signal, too.

At the railroad crossing, a sign blinks off and on.
Cars and trucks come to a stop. The signal warns
them not to cross the track because a train is coming.

Light signals are used to guide boats and ships through seaway systems. The flashing lights make different patterns. They tell the ships' crews when they can proceed through a lock or a canal and when they should stop.

Out at sea, the captain of a ship looks for a flashing light. It is a lighthouse beacon. Like the beacon fires of old, the lighthouse warns the captain that his ship is near the rocky coast. Each lighthouse flashes its own signal. Lighthouses guide ships and boats safely from one place to another.

Flares are other sight signals. They are used to signal for help. At the side of a highway a car breaks down. The driver places a flare next to her car and waits for help.

A ship is in danger at sea. The crew signals another boat by shooting a flare into the dark sky.

Often, mirrors are used to send signals, too. A camper climbs to a hillside and reflects the light off the surface of her mirror. This tells her distant companion where she can be found.

"Finish!"

"Require assistance!"

"S"

Flags are also used for signaling. Some flags show their meaning through color and design. A race car zooms by! A checkered flag signals to the driver that hc has completed the race.

A ship can use flags to send messages to other ships. Each flag signals a different message.

Sometimes the way flags are moved gives their signal. A Boy Scout moves two flags into different positions to signal letters of the alphabet to a friend. This is called semaphore signaling. When one flag is used, it is called wigwagging.

People use hand signals, too. Some hand signals are known all over the world. A parent signals to her child to quiet down.

During a football game, the referee signals the players to stop. The two teams must wait for a decision to be made on a play. Then the game can start again.

The noise in the steel mill is very loud. The workers wear headgear to protect their ears. One worker signals another worker to pick up a heavy beam.

Sign language is a system of hand signals. Sign language has been used for a very long time. American Indians used sign language when they didn't speak the same language.

Today, many deaf people use sign language to communicate. They may signal an entire word or they may spell the word using their fingers.

There are many kinds of sound signals.

A whistle is a sound signal. A woman whistles for her dog to come home.

On a playground, the teacher blows her whistle.

In the distance, a train whistle wails. "Stay off the track!" it warns.

Sirens are warning sound signals. A fire-engine siren screams down the road, warning cars and trucks to get out of the way.

Bells are sound signals, too. We hear them all day! It's early morning. An alarm clock signals that it's time to get up.

The school bell rings. It's the beginning of a school day.

A church bell rings twelve times, telling people that it's noon.

Someone presses the front doorbell to signal "Open the door."

A telephone rings.

In a theater lobby, a soft chime tells the audience that the concert is about to begin.

Sometimes bells are used as warning signals. Then they are called alarms. A fire alarm rings at the firehouse. There's a fire in town! The firefighters rush to their fire engines.

A burglar alarm goes off in a home, signaling the police. They race in their cars, hoping to catch the thief.

Bells are used as safety signals, too. On a foggy night, a harbor bell buoy rings to guide captains and their crews into the snug harbor.

Horns are used for another kind of signal. In this faraway castle, a celebration is about to begin. Horns announce the arrival of guests.

On the expressway, traffic is backed up. Drivers beep their horns to signal "Let's get moving!"

At summer camp, a horn signals that it's time to get up.

Guns are fired to signal the beginning of some races. People at the swimming meet hold their breaths. A gun is fired and swimmers dive into the water. They're off!

DOT...DOT...

"Save Our Ship!"

The most widely used sound signal is Morse code. It was invented by Samuel Morse to send messages by electric telegraph. Morse code is a combination of dots and dashes—or short and long sounds—that stand for letters of the alphabet. SOS is an international distress signal—three dots, three dashes, and three dots.

A teakettle whistles. The doorbell rings. A traffic
arrow flashes green.

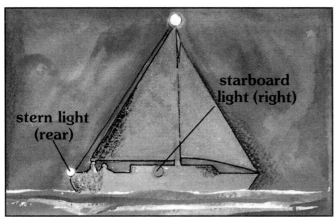

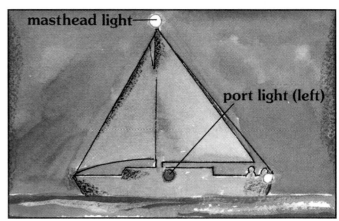

A bell buoy clangs. An airport worker uses batons to guide an airplane into position. Lights tell a boat's direction in the night.

"Good-bye!"

All of these are signals that tell us something we want to know.

MEET
GAIL GIBBONS

Gail Gibbons has written more than seventy books. She has also made the drawings for these books. Most of her books are not just stories. She writes about things that help us learn about the world. Some of her books are about trains, newspapers, animals, and holidays. She likes to travel. She often writes about the countries she visits.

AROUND THE WORLD WITH HAM RADIO

By Kenny A. Chaffin

"You're five by seven in Birmingham, England. How copy?"

"G3ENT, this is KA1VVW. Your signal's five-nine in Meriden, Connecticut. Thanks for the report. Handle here is Ian, and I'm 8 years old. Over."

"Hello, Ian. Pleased to meet you. You are the youngest ham I've ever talked to!"

Ian Delahorne loves to ham it up—on his ham radio, that is! Ian learned how to be a ham by watching his dad. He started reading his dad's ham-radio books when he was only six years old. Ian liked ham radio so much he decided to try to get his own ham license. But first, Ian had to pass an important test.

Ian Delahorne of Meriden, Connecticut, hams it up with his radio. His call letters are KA1VVW.

Ian studied hard to learn how radios work. He also learned Morse code—an alphabet of dots and dashes. By learning Morse code, Ian would be able to talk to hams all around the world!

At age 7, Ian was ready to take the test. He passed and became one of only three 7-year-old hams in the country! Since then, Ian has talked to hams in the United States, England, Bulgaria, and many other countries.

Ian says being a ham helps him learn geography and social studies. When Ian reaches a new place with his radio, he finds that place on a map. He also reads about the place. And knowing about radios helps Ian with science and math.

Ian says most kids can get a ham license if they try.

Once Ian showed his Boy Scout troop how to talk to someone over the ham radio.

"CQ, CQ, CQ, this is KA1VVW. Anyone copy?"

"KA1VVW, here is N9KEQ in Bismarck, North Dakota. You copy?"

The boys in the troop yelled excitedly. "Wow!" they said. "All the way to North Dakota! You do this all the time, Ian? How can we get licenses?"

> Would you like to find out more about ham radio?
>
> Write to: **American Radio Relay League**
> **225 Main Street**
> **Newington, CT 06111**

Dots and Dashes!

Read the secret message. Use the Ham Key to break the code.

Write the letters on the lines above the code symbols.

——— ——— ———
— • • •   •   • —

———   ———   ———   ———   ———   ———
• • • •   • —   — —   • —   — •   — • •

———   ———   ———   ———
—   — —   • •   • — •

———   ———   ———
—   • • • •   •

———   ———   ———   ———
• —   • — •   • — • •   — • •

Ham Key

a •—	g ——•	m ——	s •••	y —•—
b —•••	h ••••	n —•	t —	z ——••
c —•—•	i ••	o ———	u ••—	
d —••	j •———	p •——•	v •••—	
e •	k —•—	q ——•—	w •——	
f ••—•	l •—••	r •—•	x —••—	

97

Angel Child, Dragon Child

Written by
Michele Maria Surat •
Illustrated by
Vo-Dinh Mai

Angel Child, Dragon Child

Written by
Michele Maria Surat •
Illustrated by
Vo-Dinh Mai

My sisters skipped through the stone gate two by two. Mother was not there to skip with me. Mother was far away in Vietnam. She could not say, "Ut, my little one, be an Angel Child. Be happy in your new American school."

I hugged the wall and peeked around the corner.

Ut (oot)

A boy with fire-colored hair pointed his finger. "Pajamas!" he shouted. "They wore white pajamas to school!" The American children tilted back their long noses, laughing.

I turned away. "I want to go home to Father and Little Quang," I said.

Chi Hai's hands curved over my shoulders. "Children stay where parents place them, Ut. We stay."

Little Quang (kwang)   Chi Hai (chee hi)

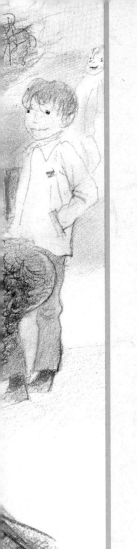

Somewhere, a loud bell jangled. I lost my sisters in a swirl of rushing children. "Pa-jaa-mas!" they teased.

Inside, the children did not sit together and chant as I was taught. Instead, they waved their hands and said their lessons one by one. I hid my hands, but the teacher called my name. "Nguyen Hoa."

Hoa is my true name, but I am Ut. Ut is my at-home name—a tender name for smallest daughter.

Nguyen Hoa (new-yen hwa)

101

"Hoa," the teacher said slowly. "Write your name, please." She pressed a chalk-piece to my hand and wrote in the air.

"I not understand," I whispered. The round-eyed children twittered. The red-haired boy poked my back.

"Stand up, Pajamas!"

I stood and bowed. *"Chao buoi sang,"* I said like an Angel Child. The children screeched like bluejays.

I sat down and flipped up my desk top, hiding my angry Dragon face.

chao buoi sang (chow bwee sung)

$\mathfrak{D}$eep in my pocket, I felt Mother's gift—a small wooden matchbox with silvery edges. I took it out and traced the *hoa-phuong* on the lid. When I tapped the tiny drawer, Mother's eyes peeked over the edge.

"I will keep you safe in here, Mother," I told her. "See? You will just fit beside the crayons."

Her listening face smiled. In my heart, I heard the music of her voice. "Do not be angry, my smallest daughter," she said. "Be my brave little Dragon."

So all day I was brave, even when the children whispered behind their hands and the clock needles ticked slowly. Finally, the bell trilled. Time for home!

hoa-phuong (hwa fung)

As soon as he saw me, Little Quang crowed, "Ut! Ut! Ut!" His laughing eyes gleamed like watermelon seeds. I dropped my books and slung him on my hip.

There he rode, tugging my hair as I sorted mint leaves and chives. Little Quang strung rice noodles from the cup hooks. Father and I laughed at this happy play.

At night, small brother curled tight beside me.
I showed him Mother's lonely face inside the matchbox.
Together we prayed, "Keep Mother safe. Send her to us
soon." With Mother's picture near, we slept like Angel
Children.

In this way, many days passed.

One day at school, small feathers floated past the frosty windows. "Mother," I whispered, "this is snow. It makes everything soft, even the angry trees with no leaves to make them pretty."

My fingers danced on the desk top while I waited for the bell. When it rang, I rushed out the door.

Outside, snowflakes left wet kisses on my cheeks. "Chi Hai!" I called. "Catch some!"

"It disappears!" she cried.

Just as Chi Hai spoke, a snowrock stung her chin. That red-haired boy darted behind the dumpster. He was laughing hard.

I tried, but I could not be a noble Dragon. Before I knew it, I was scooping up snow. My hands burned and my fingers turned red. I threw my snowrock and the laughing stopped.

Suddenly, the boy tackled me! We rolled in the snow, kicking and yelling, until the principal's large hand pinched my shoulder.

"Inside!" he thundered, and he marched us to our classroom.

"**W**e can't have this fighting. You two have to help each other," ordered the principal. He pointed at me. "Hoa, you need to speak to Raymond. Use our words. Tell him about Vietnam." Raymond glared. "And you, Raymond, you must learn to listen. You will write Hoa's story."

"But I can't understand her funny words," Raymond whined. "Anyway, I don't have a pencil."

"Use this one, then," said the principal. He slapped down a pencil, turned and slammed the door. His shoes squeegeed down the hall.

"Pajamas!" Raymond hissed. He crinkled his paper and snapped the pencil in two. He hid his head in his arms. How could I tell my story to *him*?

The clock needles blurred before my eyes. No! I *would not* be an Angel Child for this cruel-hearted boy.

But later, across the room, I heard a sniffle. Raymond's shoulders jiggled like Little Quang's when he cried for Mother.

I crept over. Gently, I tugged the sad boy's sleeve. He didn't move. "Raymond," I pleaded, "not cry. I give you cookie."

Suddenly, his head bounced up. "Hoa!" he shouted. "You said my name. You didn't use funny words." He broke off a piece of the cookie.

"I say English," I answered proudly. "And you call me Ut. Ut is my at-home name, from Vietnam."

"Okay, *Ut*," he mumbled. "But only if you tell me what's in your matchbox."

"My mother," I told him. We giggled and ate the cookie crumbs.

111

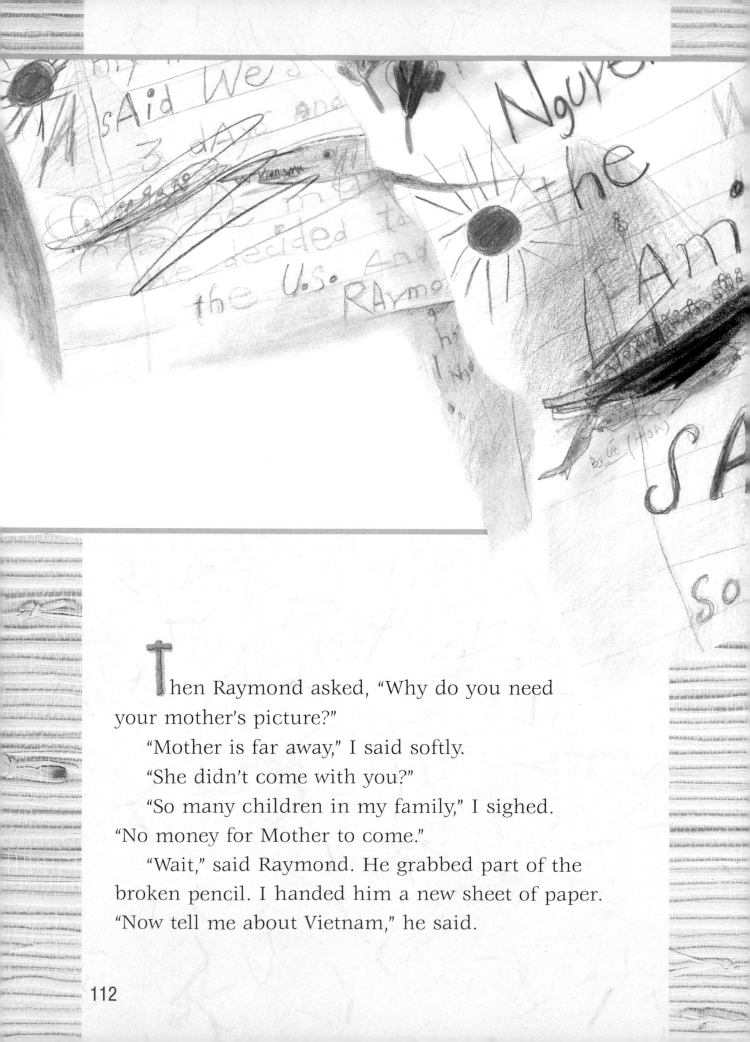

Then Raymond asked, "Why do you need your mother's picture?"

"Mother is far away," I said softly.

"She didn't come with you?"

"So many children in my family," I sighed. "No money for Mother to come."

"Wait," said Raymond. He grabbed part of the broken pencil. I handed him a new sheet of paper. "Now tell me about Vietnam," he said.

Raymond scrawled my words in black squiggles. I crayoned pictures in the margins.

When we were ready, Raymond leaned out the door. "Done!" he beamed. He waved the story like a flag.

The principal squeegeed up the hall. "You may go," said the big man.

We dashed through the stone gate together.

The next day, the principal read our story to the whole school. "These girls sailed many oceans to be here. They left behind their home, their friends, and most important of all, their mother. So now . . . "

"Ut's mother needs money for the long boat ride to America!" shouted a familiar voice. Raymond stood on his chair. "And we could have a fair and *earn* the money."

"Young man!" warned the principal.

Raymond slid down in his seat. "We could," he insisted. I hid my eyes. I held my breath. Chi Hai squeezed my hand.

"A special fair! A Vietnamese fair!" my teacher exclaimed. My eyes opened wide.

The principal's eyebrows wiggled like caterpillars. "But who will help with a Vietnamese fair?"

"Me!" cried Raymond.

"We will!" squealed the children.

"Well, what are we waiting for?" said the principal. And we all clapped for the fair.

On the special day, I wore my white *ao dai*
and welcomed everyone to our Vietnamese fair.
"Chao buoi sang," I said, bowing like an Angel Child.
"Chao buoi sang," they answered, smiling.

ao dai (ow zi)

High above our heads, our rainbow dragon floated freely. Below, Chi Hai and her friends sold rice cakes, imperial rolls and sesame cookies. Raymond popped balloons and won three goldfish. He gave one to Little Quang. "Don't eat it," he warned.

By the end of the day, we had just enough money to send to Mother. "When will she come?" I wondered.

Every day, we walked home wondering, "When will Mother come?"

We slid through icy winter. . . .

We splish-splashed through spring rain. . . .

We tiptoed barefoot through the grass, still hoping she would come.

On the last day of school, when I knew the *hoa-phuong* were blossoming in Vietnam, Raymond and I raced home faster than all my sisters. We were the first to see Father and Little Quang at the picture window, and beside them . . .

Mother!

Meet Michele Maria Surat and Vo-Dinh Mai

Vo-Dinh Mai was born in Vietnam but has lived in France and in the United States. He says, "There is a very definite message in *Angel Child, Dragon Child*: People of every country and race have the same concerns, the same problems, and the same hopes and dreams.

"Each country's history and culture is different, but human beings are basically the same no matter where they live."

Vo-Dinh Mai is also the illustrator of another children's book, *First Snow*.

Michele Maria Surat explains that *Angel Child, Dragon Child* is a make-believe story, but she got the idea from having Vietnamese students in her classes. She says, "I was impressed by my Vietnamese students who had the courage to create new lives in America, so I wanted to write about them."

Ms. Surat knows how hard it is to go to a new school. She adds, "Between the ages of nine and sixteen I went to a different school every year. My mother is Puerto Rican. My father is Czechoslovakian. I grew up with parents from two different cultures. Each culture has its own stories to tell in its own language."

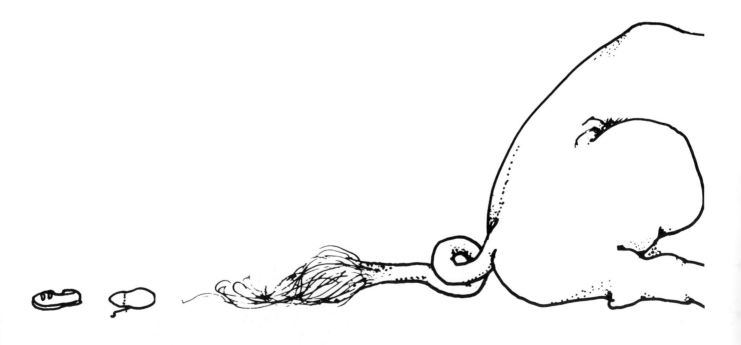

IT'S DARK IN HERE

I am writing these poems
From inside a lion,
And it's rather dark in here.
So please excuse the handwriting
Which may not be too clear.
But this afternoon by the lion's cage
I'm afraid I got too near.
And I'm writing these lines
From inside a lion,
And it's rather dark in here.

SHEL SILVERSTEIN

Unit 2

HAND in HAND

JAMAICA TAG-ALONG

By Juanita Havill

Illustrations by Anne Sibley O'Brien

Jamaica ran to the kitchen to answer the phone.
But her brother got there first.

"It's for me," Ossie said.

Jamaica stayed and listened to him talk.

"Sure," Ossie said. "I'll meet you at the court."

Ossie got his basketball from the closet. "I'm going
to shoot baskets with Buzz."

"Can I come, too?" Jamaica said. "I don't have
anything to do."

"Ah, Jamaica, call up your own friends."

"Everybody is busy today."

"I don't want you tagging along."

"I don't want to tag along," Jamaica said. "I just want to play basketball with you and Buzz."

"You're not old enough. We want to play serious ball."

Ossie dribbled his basketball down the sidewalk. Jamaica followed at a distance on her bike.

Buzz was already at the school court, shooting baskets with Jed and Maurice.

She parked her bike by the bushes and crept to the corner of the school building to watch.

That's not fair, Jamaica thought. Maurice is shorter than I am.

Pom, pa-pom, pa-pom, pom, pom.

The boys started playing, Ossie and Jed against Buzz and Maurice.

Jamaica sneaked to the edge of the court.

Maurice missed a shot and the ball came bouncing toward her. Jamaica jumped. "I've got the ball," she yelled.

"Jamaica!" Ossie was so surprised he tripped over Buzz. They both fell down.

Jamaica dribbled to the basket and tossed the ball. It whirled around the rim and flew out.

"I almost made it," Jamaica shouted. "Can I be on your team, Ossie?"

"No. N-O, Jamaica. I told you not to tag along."

"It's not fair. You let Maurice play."

"We need two on a team. Why don't you go play
on the swings and stay out of the way?"

"I still think it's not fair." Jamaica walked slowly
over to the sandlot.

She started to swing, but a little boy kept walking in front of her. His mom should keep him out of the way, Jamaica thought.

She looked up and saw a woman pushing a baby
back and forth in a stroller.

Jamaica sat down in the sand and began to
dig. She made a big pile with the wet sand from
underneath. She scooped sand from the mound to
form a wall.

"Berto help," said the little boy. **He sprinkled**
dry sand on the walls.

"Don't," said Jamaica. "You'll **just mess it up.**"
Jamaica turned her back.

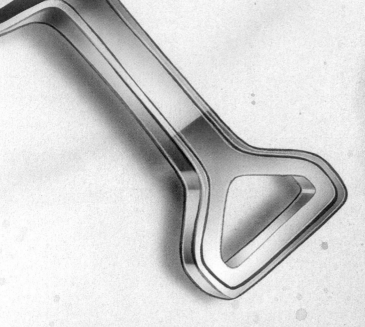

She piled the wet sand high. She made a castle with towers. She dug a ditch around the wall.

Jamaica turned to see if Berto was still there. He stood watching. Then he tried to step over the ditch, and his foot smashed the wall.

"Stay away from my castle," Jamaica said.

"Berto," the woman pushing the stroller said, "leave this girl alone. Big kids don't like to be bothered by little kids."

"That's what my brother always says," Jamaica
said. She started to repair the castle. Then she
thought, but I don't like my brother to say that.
It hurts my feelings.

Jamaica smoothed the wall. "See, Berto, like that. You can help me make a bigger castle if you're very careful."

Jamaica and Berto made a giant castle. They put water from the drinking fountain in the moat.

"Wow," Ossie said when the game was over and the other boys went home. "Need some help?"

"If you want to," Jamaica said.

Jamaica, Berto, and Ossie worked together on the castle.

Jamaica didn't even mind if Ossie tagged along.

MEET JUANITA HAVILL

Juanita Havill has been telling stories for a long time. As a young child, Ms. Havill made up stories. Her stories were important to her. They let her make believe she could do all kinds of fun things. When she grew up, she became a teacher and visited many places. But she kept on writing. She took a writing class. She found that she liked to write for children. By now, she has written many children's books. Ms. Havill says, "I write to find out what I think, to give form to thought."

MEET ANNE SIBLEY O'BRIEN

Anne Sibley O'Brien was born in Chicago, Illinois. Most of her childhood was spent in Korea. She never forgot what it was like to live in another country. She learned about many other ways of life. Today Ms. O'Brien's art shows peoples of all colors. She has also drawn pictures for another book about Jamaica. In both books she worked hard to make the people seem real. She hoped to show how the members of Jamaica's family love each other.

KIDS **HELP**ING KIDS

TAGALONGS

Dear Kids,
I have a big problem. I like to read. But every time I sit down to read, my little sister wants to play. If I don't play with my sister, she starts to cry. That's not all. My little sister follows me everywhere. Anytime I go to a friend's house, my sister wants to go too. Sometimes I just want to be alone. What should I do?

Suzi P.
Texas

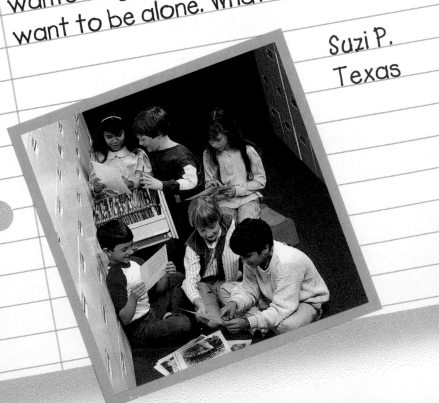

We asked our Kids Helping Kids panel about Suzi's letter. Here are their ideas.

Meredith: Talk to your sister. Explain that you can't spend all your time with her.

Ranjit: Explain that you have some work to do, or that you've just finished your chores and would like some time to relax.

Jina: Ask your parents to talk to your sister. She may listen to your parents better than she will listen to you.

Tim: Sometimes when I have a friend over, my sister wants to play ball with us. We let her play for a while, then I show her another ball game she can play by herself. She gets so interested in her game that she forgets about us.

Thomasin: Invite one of her friends over to play with her. Then you can read or do whatever you want.

Matthew: I think you should play with your sister for a while when she asks you. There are other times when you can read, like after she goes to bed.

Meredith

Ranjit

Jina

Tim

Thomasin

Matthew

An umbrella and a raincoat
Are walking and talking together.

Buson

In the fields of spring,
The nightingales sing.
To gain their friendship,
The plum blossoms have burst open
In the garden of my house.

Anonymous

r A y

Laura's new this year in school.

She acts so opposite, it seems like a rule.

If someone says yes, Laura says no.

If someone says high, Laura says low.

If you say bottom, she'll say top.

If you say go, she'll always stop.

If you say short, Laura says tall.

If you say none, she says all.

If you say beginning, Laura says end. . .

But today she asked me to be her friend.

I said maybe

But not quite yes.

Then I said, "Want to take a walk?"

And Laura said, "I guess."

Jeff Moss

MEET
ELIZABETH WINTHROP

Elizabeth Winthrop wrote *The Best Friends Club* because of what happened to her as a child. She says, "I grew up with five brothers. Like Lizzie, I always made rules, but they paid no attention to me."

Ms. Winthrop thinks friendship is important to all children. She adds, "My children were always worried about having friends. How do I get a best friend? Will I keep her or him? What's a best friend like?"

She says about her writing, "When I write, I go into myself and find out what I'm feeling."

She adds, "I love writing for children. *The Best Friends Club* is a sequel to *Lizzie and Harold*. I knew their story wasn't over, so I wrote another one."

MEET MARTHA WESTON

Martha Weston was very excited about illustrating *The Best Friends Club* because she likes Lizzie so much.

She explains, "As a child, I was really bossy and had to show everyone how to do everything. Everything had to be done the way I wanted it to be done. Lizzie is like that, and I love her because she reminds me of myself.

"When I began drawing Lizzie and Harold, I asked my daughter and her friend to model for me. I asked them to do the things that Lizzie and Harold do in the story, and I took pictures of them. I paid them ten cents each for every picture I took."

THE BEST FRIENDS CLUB

BY ELIZABETH WINTHROP

ILLUSTRATED BY MARTHA WESTON

Lizzie and Harold were best friends.
Harold taught Lizzie how to do cat's cradle.
Lizzie taught Harold how to play running bases.

Lizzie shared her trick-or-treat candy with Harold, and Harold let Lizzie ride his big red bike.

They always walked home from school together.

"Let's start a best friends club," Lizzie said one day.

"Great," said Harold. "We can meet under your porch. That will be our clubhouse."

Harold painted the sign.

It said

THE BF CLUB.

"Now write *Members Only,*" said Lizzie.

"You write it," said Harold. "My teacher says my M's are too fat."

So Lizzie wrote *Members Only.*

"Who are the members?" Harold asked.

"You and me," said Lizzie.
"That's all?"
"Yes," said Lizzie. "You can be the president and I'll be the vice-president. The president gets to write down all the rules."

"You be the president," Harold said. "Your writing is better than mine."

"All right, then I'll be president," said Lizzie. "Now we'll make up the rules."

"Rule number one," said Harold. "The club meets under Lizzie's porch."

"Right," said Lizzie. "Rule number two. Nobody else can be in the club."

"Rule number three," said Harold. He thought for a long time. "I can't think of any more."

"Rule number three," said Lizzie. "Lizzie and Harold walk home from school together every day."

"Rule number four," said Harold. "Everybody in the club knows cat's cradle."

They heard voices. Someone was walking by. They could see two pairs of feet.

"It's Christina," whispered Lizzie. "She always wears those black party shoes."

"And Douglas," Harold whispered back. "His shoelaces are always untied."

"I'm only having Nancy and Amy and Stacey to my birthday party," they heard Christina say.

"My mother said I could have my whole class," Douglas answered. "We're going to play baseball."

"Oh goody," said Harold. "That means I'll be invited to Douglas's birthday party."

"I won't," Lizzie said gloomily. She was in a different class.

The next day, Harold came out of his classroom with Douglas.

"He wants to walk home with us," Harold said to Lizzie.

"He can't," said Lizzie.

"Why not?" asked Harold.

"Harold, remember the rules. We're best friends and we always walk home together," Lizzie said. "Just you and me."

"Oh yeah," said Harold. "I forgot."

Douglas looked very sad.

"Sorry, Douglas," Harold said. "See you tomorrow."

"Douglas's ears stick out," Lizzie said on the way home.

"So what?" said Harold.

"His shoelaces are always dripping," said Lizzie.

"I don't care about that," said Harold.

"I'll meet you in the clubhouse after snacks," said Lizzie.

"I can't come today," said Harold. "My mother wants me home."

Lizzie sat in the clubhouse all by herself.

She wrote down more rules.

They said

5. Best friends don't go to other people's birthday parties.

6. People with funny ears and drippy shoelaces are not allowed in the club.

The next day, Harold came out of his classroom with Douglas again.

"Douglas asked me to play at his house," said Harold.

"*Harold,*" said Lizzie. "What about the club?"

"What club?" asked Douglas.

"None of your business," said Lizzie.

"I'll come tomorrow," said Harold. "I promise."

Lizzie watched them walk away together. She stuck out her tongue at them but Harold didn't turn around.

She went straight to the clubhouse and wrote down another rule. It said

7. Best friends don't go to other people's houses to play.

Then she threw a ball at the garage wall until suppertime.

"Douglas wants to be in the club," said Harold the next day.

"He can't be," said Lizzie. "Only best friends are allowed in this club."

She showed him all the new rules she had written down.

"This club is no fun," said Harold. "It has too many rules. I quit."

He crawled out from under the porch and walked home.

Lizzie took down his sign and put up a new one.

Douglas came down the street.

He was riding Harold's new bicycle.

Harold was chasing after him.

When Harold saw the sign, he stopped and read it.

"What does it say?" asked Douglas.

"It says, 'Lizzie's Club. Nobody Else Allowed,'"
Harold said.

Harold leaned over and looked at Lizzie. "You can't
have a club with only one person," he said.

"*I* can," said Lizzie.

"A three-person club is more fun," said Harold.
"Douglas knows how to do cat's cradle."

"But he's not a best friend,"
said Lizzie.

"It'll be a different kind of club," said Harold.
"We'll make up a new name."
"Maybe," said Lizzie.
She sat under the porch and watched them.
First they played bicycle tag.
Then they threw the ball at her garage wall.

"Want to play running bases?" Lizzie asked.

"I don't know how," said Douglas.

"I'll teach you," said Lizzie.

They took turns being the runner. Lizzie was the fastest.

Douglas whispered something to Harold.

"Douglas wants you to come to his birthday party," said Harold.

Then Lizzie whispered something to Harold.

"Lizzie says yes," Harold said to Douglas.

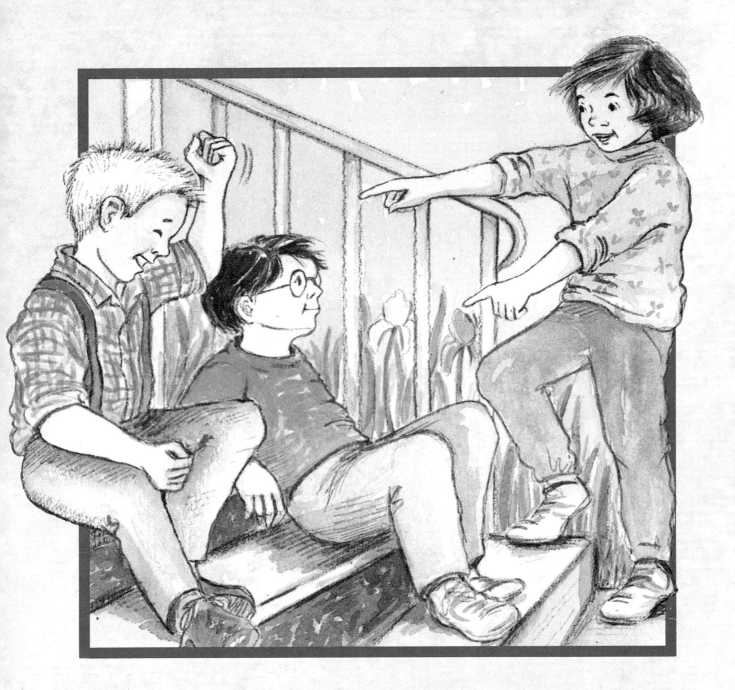

"And I've thought of a new name for the club," said Lizzie. "Douglas can be in it too."

"Oh boy!" said Douglas.

"You can be the first member. I am the president and Harold is the vice-president," said Lizzie.

"That's okay with me," said Harold.

"Me too," said Douglas.

It was getting dark.

Douglas went home for supper.

Lizzie crawled back under the porch. She tore up her sign and her list of rules.

"What's the new name for the club?" Harold asked.

"I'll show you," said Lizzie.

She sat down and wrote in great big letters
THE NO RULES CLUB.

Harold smiled.

He stuck up the sign with a thumbtack.

Then they both went upstairs to Lizzie's house
for supper.

FINDING A WAY

I'd like you for a friend.
I'd like to find the way
Of asking you to be my friend.
I don't know what to say.

What would you like to hear?
What is it I can do?
There has to be some word, some look
Connecting me to you.

MYRA COHN LIVINGSTON

173

174

DOWN THE WALK

We're racing, racing down the walk,
Over the pavement and round the block.
We rumble along till the sidewalk ends—
Felicia and I and half our friends.
Our hair flies backward. It's whish and whirr!
She roars at me and I shout at her
As past the porches and garden gates
We rattle and rock
On our roller skates.

Phyllis McGinley

OUR SOCCER LEAGUE

BY CHUCK SOLOMON

WE'RE THE FALCONS.
WE PLAY SOCCER!

Today the game is with our friends, the Sluggers. They wear blue shirts.

First everyone stretches.

Then we practice.

In soccer, you dribble the ball with your feet.

You pass to your teammates.

And you try to kick the ball through the goal, if you can.

Goalies need practice, too. They stop the other team from scoring, and they're the only players on the field who can touch the ball with their hands.

Falcons' goal

X Falcons (white shirts)

Out-of-bounds

o Sluggers (blue shirts)

Sluggers' goal

It's game time!

The coaches give us our positions for the opening kickoff.

The Sluggers kick off and burst downfield. They charge to the goal. There's a goal kick.

Defense! Our goalie, Toby, makes a save. Toby throws it out, and we have the ball.

Eric dribbles to midfield . . . with the Sluggers in pursuit. Eric passes . . .

but a Slugger intercepts! He gets his foot behind the ball . . . and boots it!

The Sluggers have the ball.

But then it is kicked out-of-bounds. Whenever a team puts the ball out, the other team throws it back in.

Moira throws it in for us.

"Don't use your hands, Johnny!"

Eric booms it.

Score! It's one to nothing, Falcons.

Teams	1st half	2nd half	Final
Falcons	1		
Sluggers			

But not for long.

The Sluggers bounce right back and tie the game.

It's now one to one.

Teams	1st half	2nd half	Final
Falcons	1		
Sluggers	1		

The score is still tied at one to one when the coaches call halftime.

Whew! It feels good to take a break.

After a ten-minute rest . . .

we're back to the game!

184

We charge down to the Slugger's goal.

Olivier's kick is wide . . .

and the Sluggers take the ball.

185

Here comes our defense
at midfield.
 The two players collide.

 It's anybody's ball.

 The Sluggers and Falcons
battle for the ball.

 The ball goes up . . .

Joely kicks it . . .

Oh, no! "Hand ball!" Since a Slugger touched the ball, we get a free kick.

Jonathan booms it and we have control again.

No one scored, and the clock is running out. Only five minutes are left in the game.

5:00

190

2:00

Out-of-bounds on a header.

Ted throws it in.

The Sluggers boot the ball
into the open field.

1:00

John's set . . . boom!

Score! It's two to one,
Sluggers!

195

We try our best to tie the score . . .

but the clock runs out.

0:00

Teams	1st half	2nd half	Final
Falcons	1	0	1
Sluggers	1	1	2

The Sluggers celebrate . . .

and we give ourselves a cheer.

When you play a great game . . .

everybody wins!

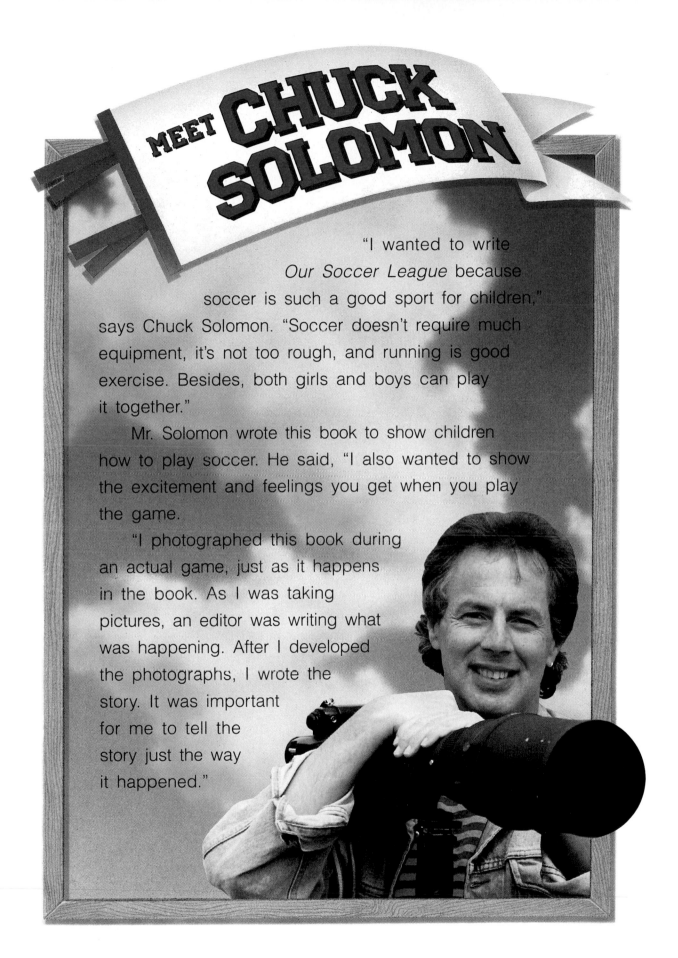

MEET CHUCK SOLOMON

"I wanted to write *Our Soccer League* because soccer is such a good sport for children," says Chuck Solomon. "Soccer doesn't require much equipment, it's not too rough, and running is good exercise. Besides, both girls and boys can play it together."

Mr. Solomon wrote this book to show children how to play soccer. He said, "I also wanted to show the excitement and feelings you get when you play the game.

"I photographed this book during an actual game, just as it happens in the book. As I was taking pictures, an editor was writing what was happening. After I developed the photographs, I wrote the story. It was important for me to tell the story just the way it happened."

TRUE BUT STRANGE

By Christina Wilsdon

Everything on these pages is true. Honest. We wouldn't kid you.

Sock-er?

Pele, one of the greatest soccer players in history, practiced his moves as a kid. He didn't have a soccer ball, so he used an odd "foot" ball: a sock full of rags!

Having a Ball

Usually only one soccer ball is used in a whole soccer game. But one pro football game can use up as many as 24 footballs. And a baseball game might use up 100 or more baseballs!

200

Bad Sports

King Edward II banned soccer in England about 650 years ago because the game was too noisy. Other kings banned soccer because they wanted people to spend more time learning how to use a bow and arrow!

World Pup

The team that wins the World Cup takes home a beautiful trophy. In 1966, someone stole this trophy. A dog named Pickles found it while digging in a garbage heap!

Town Ball

Soccer games in England 800 years ago were really big deals. Teams were made up of whole towns! A team could have more than 100 people.

BY KATHLEEN M. MULDOON
Illustrated by Linda Shute

Princess Pooh

$\mathcal{M}$y big sister is ten years old. Her name is Penelope Marie Piper, but everyone calls her Penny. Everyone except me. I, Patty Jean Piper, call her Princess Pooh. No one knows I call her that, but it's the perfect name for her. All day she just sits on her throne with wheels and tells everybody in the whole world what to do.

When we go shopping at the mall, Princess Pooh rides on her throne while Dad wheels her around. She smiles and waves like she's some kind of movie star. Mom carries the Princess's crutches and I, Patty Jean the Servant, carry packages. Sometimes there are so many I look like a box with legs.

Everyone loves the Princess. Grandma and Grandpop and all the aunts and uncles and cousins in our family hug her and say how sweet and wonderful she is. Then they look at me and say I am growing like a weed. That's the way it has been for a million years. The Princess is a flower. I, plain old Patty Jean, am a weed.

Once we went to a carnival. Princess Pooh
watched me ride a hundred times on the roller
coaster. It was fun, but it would have been better
with a friend. I almost wished the Princess could
ride with me. Then I tried to win a pink stuffed
poodle. I spent all my allowance and threw a
thousand balls, but I couldn't knock down the
bottles. When we left, the man handed Princess
Pooh a yellow stuffed poodle with a diamond
collar! That's how it is. Everyone gives her things.

My school is a hundred years old. It is so far from my house I have to ride for hours on a school bus to get there. Princess Pooh goes to the new school right across the street. She can wheel herself there in one second.

If it rains, Dad carries her and her throne to his car and gives her a one-second ride. I, Patty Jean, wear an icky yellow raincoat and stand in mud puddles, waiting for the bus.

Saturday is chore day. Mom mows the lawn. Dad washes clothes and cleans the garage. Then he brings the clean clothes to the Princess, and she folds them into piles on the table. I, Patty Jean the Maid, clean the bathroom.

One Saturday, Mom asked me to fold clothes because Princess Pooh had therapy. I sat at the table pretending I was the Princess. I folded the clothes very fast and put them in perfect stacks. When the Princess came home, I waited for Mom to tell her to clean the bathroom. But Mom put her right to bed because she was tired. So I, exhausted Patty Jean, had to clean the bathroom, too.

It is summer now. All my friends have gone to camp—everyone except me. Mom says there's no money to send me to camp because the Princess got new braces for her legs.

Princess Pooh doesn't need them anyway because all she does is sit. She only takes little tiny walks, like when she has to go to the bathroom at a restaurant and her wheelchair won't fit through the door. Mom says she walks at therapy, too, but I've never seen her do it.

After dinner I go outside. The Princess is in the hammock reading a book.

"Do you want to make a puppet show?" I ask.

"No, thanks," she says in her princess voice. "I'm going to read lots of books so I can win a prize in the summer reading program."

I don't feel like reading, but I get a book anyway and look at the pictures. I am finished in one minute.

"This book is boring," I say. "Let's play with puppets now." The Princess doesn't answer. I look over at the hammock—there she is, asleep.

Behind the tree is the throne. Seeing it empty gives me the best idea anyone in the whole world has ever had. Today I, Patty Jean, will be the Princess!

I sit on the throne. It is covered with cushions and feels like a cloud.

"I will rest on my golden throne for the whole evening," I say. I imagine all the people in my kingdom, looking at me and loving their beautiful new princess.

The throne is hard to wheel on the grass, so I get up and pull it to the front yard. "Now I will spend *every minute* on the throne," I say.

I decide to ride to the Princess's school. There is a nice, steep little hill on the grass near the sidewalk. Maybe it would be fun to ride down it. I sit down and give the throne a good, hard push.

PLOP! The throne dumps me out on the sidewalk and lands upside down on top of me. My knee has a tiny cut on it, but it doesn't hurt much. Still, I'm glad no one is around to laugh. I wonder if Princess Pooh ever fell when she was learning. I put the throne rightside up and get back on it. Then I ride to the corner. I go down the low place on the curb so I can cross the street.

215

When the light turns green, I push the wheels as fast as I can. I make it to the island in the middle, but then the light turns red again.

Cars and trucks and buses rush by. I cover my face so I will not see myself go SPLAT.

Finally, the traffic stops and the light is green again. I finish crossing the street. I push the throne up the low place at the crosswalk. It is hard to go uphill, but I do it. I wheel down the sidewalk. I've been pushing so hard I feel like both my arms are broken.

Some grown-ups are walking toward me. They look at me and my throne, and then they turn away fast, like I do when I'm watching a scary movie. Does this happen to Princess Pooh?

Some boys are playing on the sidewalk and will not move out of my way. "Why don't you go over me, Wheel Legs?" says one of them. All his friends laugh. "I'll beat you up!" I yell, but they just laugh some more and run away.

I see an ice-cream truck on the school playground. Lots of big kids are crowded around it. I make a shortcut across the baseball field, but by the time I get there and take some money out of my pocket, the worst thing in the world has happened. Great big raindrops have started falling over everything! SLAM goes the window on the truck. The children squeal and run away.

The man drives off and I'm alone on my wet throne.

The rain comes faster and faster. I think about running home, too, but I can't leave the throne out in the rain. Besides, I am still the Princess. I'm spending every minute on my throne, even if I do get wet! So I push harder and harder. When I get back to the baseball field, I can see it's a muddy mess. The wheels of the throne sink down, down, down. They stop turning. My hands are covered with mud. I jump off the throne, and my new sandals sink, too. My feet go with them. By the time I pull the throne out, I am wetter and colder than I have ever been in my whole life. I, Princess Patty Jean, am a royal mess. It is definitely time to quit sitting on the throne.

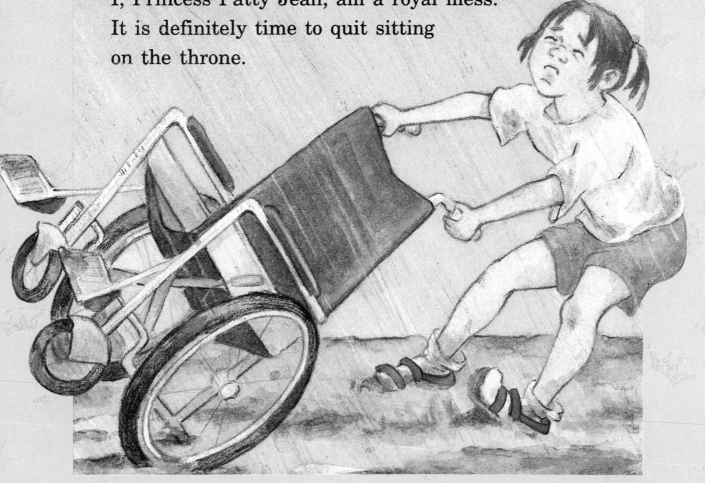

The rain stops. Across the street there is a rainbow. I notice Dad standing in our front yard. He is calling and calling, but the cars and trucks are so noisy I can't hear him. Mom is walking up the street, looking around. I drag the muddy throne across the rest of the field to the sidewalk.

Then I cross the street. When Mom sees me, she runs and holds out her arms. Dad is right behind her. "I didn't mean to mess up the throne. I'm sorry," I say.

"Throne?" says Mom. "Oh, the *wheelchair*. We thought you were lost!"

"You weren't looking for the chair?" I say.

"Patty Jean, we were looking for *you*." Mom hugs me some more. "You shouldn't have taken Penny's chair. But we're so glad you're back!"

Mom washes me in the bathtub and puts me to bed just like she does for Penny. After Dad and Mom say good-night and turn out the lights, I lie there thinking.

"Penny," I whisper. "Are you awake?"

"Uh-huh."

"Do you like walking better than sitting?"

"Well," she says, "walking makes me awful tired, but so does pushing my wheelchair.

I guess I like the wheelchair best because I can do things with my hands while I sit. When I use my crutches, I can't."

"How can you smile all the time when you're in that yucky chair?"

"It's not yucky," says Penny. "It takes me places I can't go if I just have my crutches."

That makes me think some more. "I'm sorry I took your chair," I say.

"That's all right. Just go to sleep now."

But I'm wide awake. I lie there and wish very hard that my sister will always be able to do things that make her happy. I think that maybe Princess isn't a good name for her, after all. Maybe it's nicer that she's just Penelope Marie and that I am her sister, Patty Jean Piper.

Meet
KATHLEEN M. MULDOON

Kathleen M. Muldoon knows what it is like to be physically challenged—on one leg, she wears a brace, and on the other, an artificial leg. Talking to children, she began to realize what it's like to be a brother or sister of someone like herself. She found that these children often get pushed aside because their brother or sister needs so much attention. So Ms. Muldoon decided to write a story from the sister's point of view.

Children ask Ms. Muldoon how she came up with the name "Princess Pooh." She says, "I thought of the name 'Princess Pooh' because *pooh* is a word children love to say and hear. It's like saying 'you're not so great,' so I thought it'd be a perfect nickname for the sister."

Meet
LINDA SHUTE

"What made me want to create the pictures for *Princess Pooh?* It was the voice of Patty Jean I heard speaking from the typewritten manuscript. She sounded like a spunky, funny, and thoughtful person I'd like to know. I felt the story is as much about being sisters as it is about using a wheelchair, and I tried to show that in my pictures."

Since Hanna Moved Away

The tires on my bike are flat.
The sky is grouchy gray.
At least it sure feels like that
Since Hanna moved away.

Chocolate ice cream tastes like prunes.
December's come to stay.
They've taken back the Mays and Junes
Since Hanna moved away.

Flowers smell like halibut.
Velvet feels like hay.
Every handsome dog's a mutt
Since Hanna moved away.

Nothing's fun to laugh about.
Nothing's fun to play.
They call me, but I won't come out
Since Hanna moved away.

JUDITH VIORST

Unit 3

NATURE'S WAY

COME A TIDE

Story by George Ella Lyon

Pictures by Stephen Gammell

Last March it snowed
and then it rained
for four days and nights.

"It'll come a tide,"
my grandma said.

And sure enough,
when all the creeks
rushed down to the river
like kinfolks coming home,

it did.

It washed away
little naked gardens
on Clover Fork

pigs and chickens
on Martins Fork

and a whole front porch
on Poor Fork.

234

We stood on our bridge
and watched them swirl by.
Ooo-eee! Ooo-eee! cried the pigs.
The river nudged the bridge bottom.

Still we boasted,
"It won't flood us."

But we left our radios crackling
that night when we went to sleep.

The warning whistle
didn't have to blow twice.

Cloudburst! the radio said.
Wall of water coming down!

In five minutes
we'd jumped in our clothes
and were outside headed for the truck.

"Did you hear the whistle?
Do you want to go with us?"
Mama called to our
neighbor, Mrs. Mac.

"Joe won't go
till he finds his teeth
so I've put a pot of coffee on."

239

"Did you hear the whistle?
Do you want to go with us?"
Mama called to the Cains across the street.

"I can't catch Donald!" John yelled back.

"It's that duck," his mother hollered.
"John has to save the one thing that swims.
Don't stall on our account."

241

"Did you hear the whistle?
Do you want to go with us?"
Mama called to Papa Bill next door.

"I heard it, honey.
But I've got me a boat
and I'm aiming to find the oars."

Rain came down like curtains
as we drove up Grandma's hill.

She fed us warmed-over biscuits
and coffee stout as a post.
Then she sent us to bed.

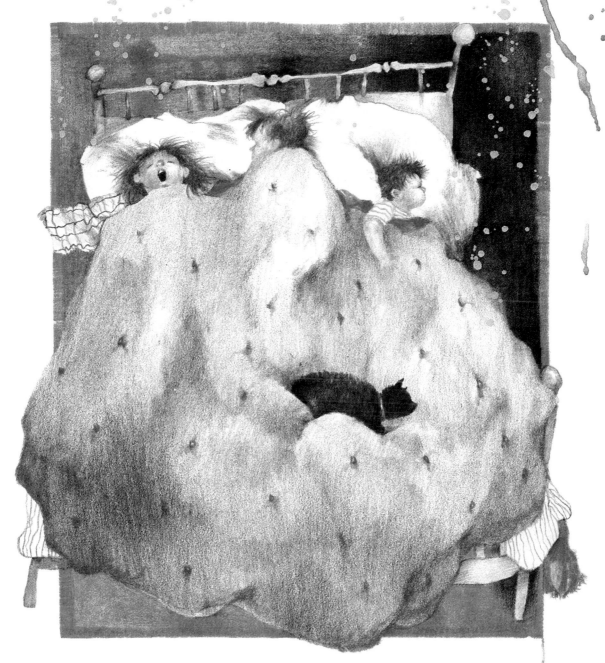

When light flooded in
and I was asleep,
Daddy went out scouting.

"Water up to the piano keys
but the house is solid."

"What do we do now?"

"If it was me," Grandma said,
"I'd make friends with a shovel."

And we did.

The Macs, the Cains, Papa Bill:
next day everyone was shoveling.
Soggy furniture and mud-mapped rugs
made mountains in front of each house.

"It got us this time,"
we had to admit, taking
lunch at the rescue wagon.

But we dug and hauled,
we scrubbed and crawled
to find our buried treasure.

Now we'll be fine,
except in spring
when the snow and rain
come together.

Then I'll hold my breath
and hope Grandma won't say,
"Children, it'll come a tide."

254

Meet
GEORGE ELLA LYON

George Ella Lyon was born and raised in Harlan, Kentucky, in the rural hills of the Appalachian Mountains. *Come a Tide* was based on the real events and people where she grew up.

In 1977, there really was water "up to the piano keys" of her parents' house. Ms. Lyon says that all the neighbors in the story are real—John really tried to catch his duck, Donald; Papa Bill was looking for the oars to his boat; and Joe wouldn't go until he found his teeth.

"The hard part of writing the story," she said, "was trying to figure out what to leave out.

"As I began writing, I was flooded with memories. I wrote down everything, and then searched for the events that made a story.

"Books come out of people's lives, and you write about what you know," Ms. Lyon said. "We breathe in experience and breathe out stories."

Meet
STEPHEN GAMMELL

Hello everybody,

So often floods are terrible. Belongings are lost or damaged, homes are wrecked, and animals are swept away. Saddest of all is when someone drowns. But *Come a Tide* is about people and animals getting by in spite of the flood. They're even having fun!

You see that the pigs are especially having fun. And when all those folks stand on the bridge and look up at the rain, do you think they care about getting wet? Not a bit. That's just part of the fun. It's a nice evening for Papa Bill to take the dog for a boat ride. And a fine time to go visit Grandma! They are making the best of it. Do you do that?

I drew the pictures with regular old colored pencils on smooth heavy paper. All the rain, the splashes, and splotches I did with watercolor. I wanted some of the pages to look wet—like this book was left out in the rain. What do you think?

Your friend,

Stephen Gammell

WHAT floats?

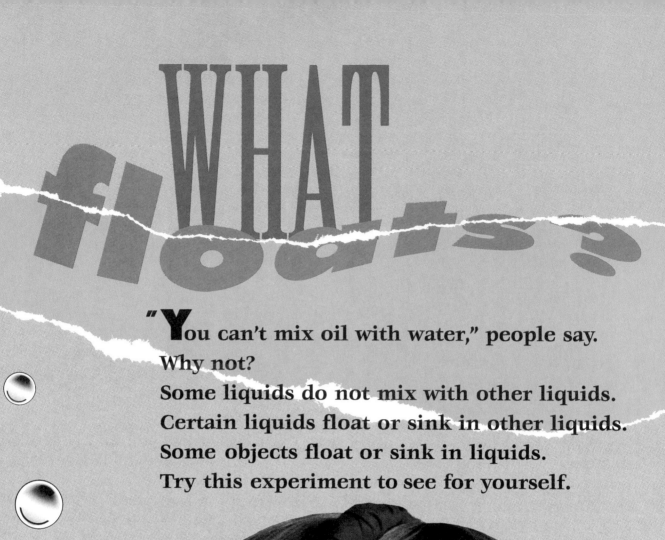

"You can't mix oil with water," people say.
Why not?
Some liquids do not mix with other liquids.
Certain liquids float or sink in other liquids.
Some objects float or sink in liquids.
Try this experiment to see for yourself.

1 Pour the syrup into the bottom of the container.

You will need:
- ○ Clear, tall container
- ○ Syrup
- ○ Cooking oil
- ○ Water
  with red food coloring
- ○ Rubbing alcohol
  with blue food coloring
- ○ Grape
- ○ Cork
- ○ Plastic building block

2 Pour in the same amount of cooking oil. It floats on the syrup.

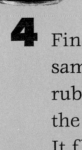

3 Now add the same amount of water. It sinks through the oil but floats on the syrup.

4 Finally, add the same amount of rubbing alcohol, the lightest liquid. It floats on the oil.

5 Now add the plastic building block, the cork and the grape in the container.

259

APRIL RAIN SONG

Let the rain kiss you.
Let the rain beat upon your head with silver liquid drops.
Let the rain sing you a lullaby.

The rain makes still pools on the sidewalk.
The rain makes running pools in the gutter.
The rain plays a little sleep-song on our roof at night—

And I love the rain.

Langston Hughes

COLORES DE CARACOL

Colores de caracol
arco iris en el cielo
es la bandera del sol.

The rainbow showing
through the rain
says the sun
will shine again.

Ernesto Galarza

The Sun, the Wind

The Sun, the Wind and the Rain

Lisa Westberg Peters · Illustrated by Ted Rand

by Lisa Westberg Peters
Illustrated by Ted Rand

and the Rain

This is the story of two mountains. The earth made one. Elizabeth in her yellow sun hat made the other.

The earth made its mountain millions of years ago.
It began as a pool underground, first fiery hot and soft,
then cold and rock-hard.

Elizabeth made hers on the beach today with
bucketsful of wet sand.

Eons passed. The earth cracked and shifted until
the rock of its mountain slowly rose.

Elizabeth quickly piled her sand high. She patted it
smooth all the way around.

The earth mountain sparkled against the sky.
Furry animals walked in its lush green valleys.

Elizabeth's mountain stood almost as tall as she,
with twigs for trees and pebbles for animals. Elizabeth
was proud of her fine sand mountain.

The sun beat down, day after day, year after year, on the earth mountain's sharp peaks. The wind howled through its canyons.

Elizabeth's mountain baked in the afternoon heat.
The breeze loosened a few grains of sand and blew them
into Elizabeth's eyes and hair.

Countless rainstorms pounded the earth mountain.
The water seeped into its rocks, making them crumble,
then tumble into small streams.

An afternoon shower blew in suddenly and Elizabeth
watched as the water began to destroy the mountain
she had worked so hard to build. Her tears fell as freely
as the rain.

The small streams rushed together to become a
raging river. The river gouged a deep valley. It ground
the earth mountain's rough rocks into smooth pebbles.

Elizabeth could see the rain carving little valleys
into her mountain. Tiny rivers carried the sand down
the beach.

As the river flowed away from the earth mountain,
it ground pebbles into sand and dumped the sand on a
broad plain. Then it emptied into the sea.

Elizabeth saw the sand from her mountain spread
silently into small fans. She wiped away her tears.

In just a blink of earth time, the earth mountain
traded rocks for sand, jagged peaks for flat layers.

After a few minutes, the shower was over. Elizabeth's mountain was just a bump on the beach.

The thick and heavy layers of sand sank down, down,
down into the earth until they were squeezed into layers
of sandstone.

Elizabeth scooped up a handful of sand from one of the small fans on the beach. She smiled. It was wet and hard—just right. This time she hurried, for the sun was dropping in the sky.

The earth cracked and shifted again. Bending and
breaking, the sandstone layers slowly rose to become
a new mountain.

Elizabeth finished her new sand mountain. She
brushed sand off her hands, picked up her bucket, and
walked back up the beach.

Elizabeth is walking on the new earth mountain.
She steps carefully up the steep path from the beach.
When she stops to rest, she sees a smooth mound
of sand far below. It looks very small.

As she turns to leave, Elizabeth reaches out to touch the sandstone wall. Tiny grains of sand fall on her shoulders.

She brushes them off and watches them fall to the
ground, where they will stay for just a while . . .
in the sun, the wind and the rain.

Meet
Lisa Westberg Peters

Lisa Westberg Peters wanted to write a book for children that would explain geology and how mountains change over time.

"I was lucky enough to take some good geology courses and several unforgettable trips into the mountains," she said. Then she visited a mountain along the coast in Washington State and wrote the story that became *The Sun, the Wind and the Rain.*

Meet
Ted Rand

Ted Rand says the mountain painted on the cover of *The Sun, the Wind and the Rain* is Mt. Rainier in the Cascade Range in Washington State. He says that the beach and shoreline are very much like those on Puget Sound and along the Pacific Coast.

"I'd like to encourage young readers to draw and enjoy the fun of it. Drawing is a second language to me, and I hope it becomes that to you," Mr. Rand says.

287

Until I Saw the SEA

Until I saw the sea
I did not know
that wind
could wrinkle water so.

I never knew
that sun
could splinter a whole sea of blue.

Nor
did I know before,
a sea breathes in and out
upon a shore.

Lilian Moore

THE WATER-GO-ROUND

Oh, the sea makes the clouds,
    And the clouds make the rain,
And the rain rains down
    On the mighty mountain chain;

Then the silver rivers race
    To the green and easy plain—
Where they hurry, flurry, scurry
    Till they reach the sea again,

And the sea makes the clouds,
    And the clouds make the rain . . .

Dennis Lee

Among the Sierra Nevada Mountains. Albert Bierstadt, 1868 NMAA

LLAMA AND THE GREAT FLOOD

**A folk tale from Peru
by Ellen Alexander**

The Quechua people of Peru say that during ancient times, before the coming of the god Viracocha, this world reached a point at which it was about to end. A certain llama who was living high up in the Andes Mountains knew what was about to happen. He had a dream in which he saw the sea overflow and flood the whole world.

This dream upset the llama so that he could not eat.
He just walked around day after day, crying.

He acted this way even though his thoughtful
owner had given him a beautiful meadow to graze in.

The llama soon began growing thin, and his owner worried about him and then started to become angry.

Finally, the man threw an ear of corn at the llama and shouted, "Why don't you eat, you foolish animal?

"I allow you to graze in this beautiful meadow and you just stand there and cry!"

The llama looked at him and with great sadness in his voice answered in the man's language, "It is YOU who are the fool!

"Don't you know what is happening? Within five days the sea will overflow!

"Yes, it's true! The world will be destroyed!"

297

The man was frightened, and he cried out to the llama, "What will become of us? How can we save ourselves?"

The llama answered, "Let us go to the top of Willka Qutu. There we will be safe. But bring enough food for five days."

The man hurried home to tell his wife and gather food.
Then the family hurried off to the highest mountain.

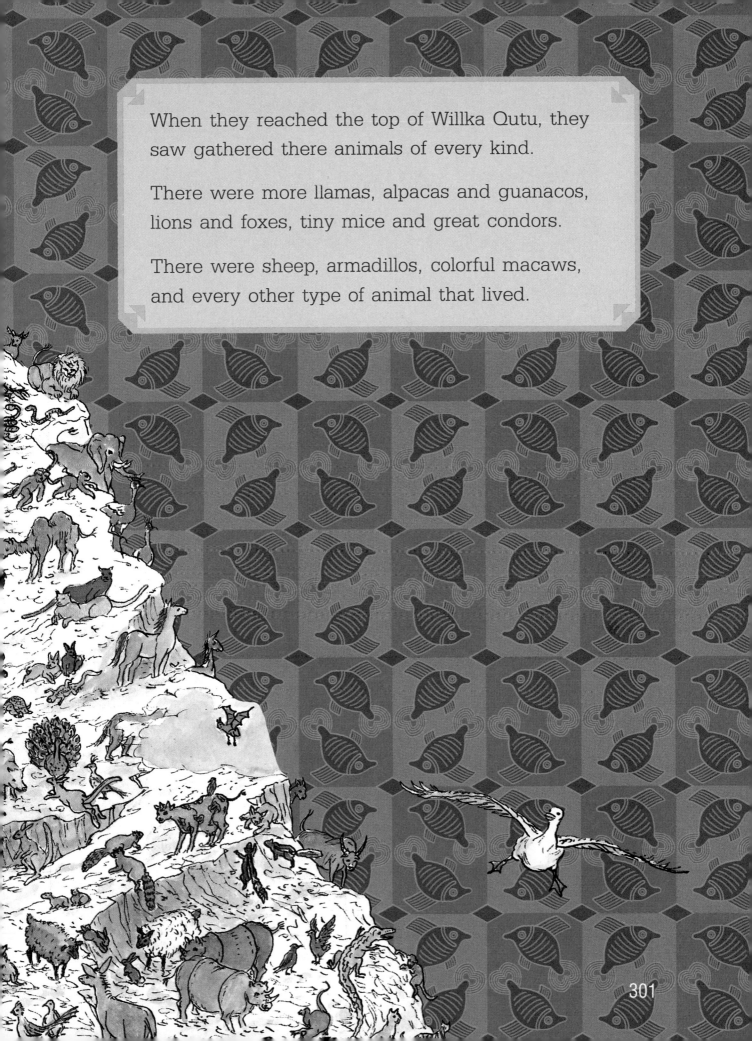

When they reached the top of Willka Qutu, they saw gathered there animals of every kind.

There were more llamas, alpacas and guanacos, lions and foxes, tiny mice and great condors.

There were sheep, armadillos, colorful macaws, and every other type of animal that lived.

Almost at once the sea began to overflow and they all remained stranded there.

The sea covered all the other mountain peaks. Only the top of Willka Qutu remained above water.

It is said that the water even reached the fox's tail and turned it black. It is still that color today.

At the end of five long, cold days, the sea went down again and everything began to dry out.

When the sea had gone all the way down, it could be seen that there were no more people or animals left in the world.

Except for those people and animals who were watching all of this from the top of Willka Qutu.

Slowly, they began climbing down, until they stood once more in the meadows and valleys.

The people began rebuilding their house of stone, and the corral for their llama. They planted corn and potatoes.

Soon many new people and animals were born into the world, and all were children of those on Willka Qutu.

The Andean people still speak of the great flood, and they believe that it was Willka Qutu and the llama who saved them from destruction.

Meet
ELLEN ALEXANDER

Ellen Alexander has traveled to South America many times. She hikes or rides horseback into the mountains and sketches and paints what she sees.

Before she left on one trip, she read a myth about a llama who saved people from a great flood. Then she visited the mountain of Willka Qutu, where the people in the myth were saved, and decided to write a book about it.

"I want to show North American children the beauty that can be found in another culture," Ms. Alexander says.

311

An Interview with Reporter
JOAN LITTLE
of the *St. Louis Post-Dispatch*

Joan Little is a newspaper reporter. She works for the *St. Louis Post-Dispatch*. She usually reports school news. But back in June 1993, it rained and rained. Then two great rivers near St. Louis—the Mississippi and the Missouri—overflowed their banks and flooded St. Louis. Deep water spread for miles and miles. The city and much of the land around it was flooded for more than two months. Reporters came from all over the country and the world to cover the great flood. Many reporters agreed it was the biggest story they had ever written about.

Q **How did you get the information you needed to write about the flood?**

A I traveled around South St. Louis by car, foot and sometimes boat. My job was to talk to as many people as I could to find out what was happening. Another reporter told me she had seen people in boats in a supermarket. They were sailing around the store, shopping for food! I also talked with emergency workers on the levees. Levees are high walls made of dirt, reinforced with sandbags, that keep the river from flooding over its banks. Many levees were leaking. To see where they were leaking, I hopped into the giant bucket of an earth moving machine. The driver raised the bucket high up over the levees.

Q What other things did you find out?

A Many people had to leave their homes. Sometimes they had to leave their pets behind. Later, rescue workers saved their pets and brought them to a park. I saw lots of cats and dogs and a whole flock of birds. People came to look for their pets. They were very happy when they found each other!

Q How did you feel about the flood?

A Sometimes it was scary. The force of the flood was very strong. Houses were washed away. Huge tanks where cooking gas is stored broke loose. They were bobbing around in the river. Firefighters were very worried. They thought the tanks might blow up. Special workers came from all over the country to save the gas tanks. To be safe, people in a large part of the city had to leave their homes until the tanks were fixed.

Q **What do you remember most about covering this story?**

A I wrote a special story about going to see the farmhouse where I grew up. That was flooded, too. It was a few miles away from St. Louis. I got there by boat and truck. There was so much water everywhere! It was overwhelming to see water filling up the basement and nearly reaching the first floor as well. It was unreal, seeing everything you grew up with under water.

Q **How did you become a reporter?**

A My Dad was a farmer. He was always interested in current events. He got both St. Louis newspapers, the *Globe-Democrat* and the *Post-Dispatch*. I always liked newspapers and reading. So, when I went to college, I studied journalism. I always wanted to be a reporter!

WATER

Water is a magic potion,
    it can fill a glass, an ocean,
raging river, tiny tear,
    drops of dew that disappear.
Water often spells surprises
    with its changing forms and sizes,
rain and snow, ponds and brooks,
    water has so many looks,
sounds and moods and colors—yet
    in every shape, it's always WET!

Joan Bransfield Graham

A Curve in

by Ann Cameron

illustrated
by Ann Strugnell

the River

This is something I learned in school: The whole body is mostly water.

We think we're solid, but we're not. You can tell sometimes from your blood and tears and stuff that what you're like inside isn't what you're like outside, but usually you'd never know.

Also, the whole earth is mostly water—three-quarters ocean. The continents are just little stopping places. And using water—streams and rivers and oceans—anybody could put a message in a bottle and send it all the way around the world.

319

That was my secret project.

I had a bottle with a cork. I had paper and a ballpoint pen. I wrote a message: *Whoever finds this bottle, please write or call me and tell me where you found it.*

I put down my address and phone number. Then I corked the bottle and carried it down to the river.

I threw the bottle as far out as I could. It splashed, bobbed up and floated. I watched it go out of sight.

I kept thinking about my secret project.

Maybe my bottle was on the way to Hawaii.

Maybe it was on the way to France.

Maybe it was on the way to China.

Maybe I would write letters to the person who found it, and we would become friends. I would go visit the person where he or she lived.

I could see myself in Rio de Janeiro, dancing in the streets.

I could see myself in India, riding on an elephant.

I could see myself in Africa, taming wild lions.

A week went by.

I wondered how long I'd have to wait before I heard from the person who got my bottle. It might be months.

Maybe my bottle would go to the North Pole and be found stuck in the ice by Eskimo hunters. Then I realized it might lie in the ice for years before it was found. Somebody might phone or write me, and I would even have forgotten about my bottle.

I decided I should write a note to myself and hide it in my desk, where I would find it when I grew up, so I could remind myself about the bottle then.

Dear Old Julian, I wrote. *Remember the bottle you threw in the river?* And then I put down the day and the year that I threw it in.

I had just finished hiding this message in the back of my desk when the phone rang.

It was Gloria.

"Julian, I have some news!" she said.

"Oh, really?" I said. Nothing could be important news that wasn't about my bottle.

"Julian," Gloria said, "it's about your bottle with the message—I found it!"

She sounded happy. I wasn't. My bottle was supposed to travel around the world.

"Julian?" Gloria said.

I didn't answer.

All that water to travel! All those countries to see! The whole world full of strangers! And where did my stupid bottle go?

To Gloria's house!

"Julian?" Gloria said. "Are you still there?"

I couldn't talk. I was too disgusted.
I hung up.

Gloria came looking for me.

"Tell her I'm not here," I said to Huey.

Huey went to the door. "Julian says he's not
here," Huey said.

"Oh," Gloria said. She went away.

In a couple of days my father
started noticing.

"I haven't seen Gloria lately," he said.

"I don't want to see her," I said.

"Why?" my father said.

"Because."

Then I decided to tell my father about the
bottle and how Gloria found it. It didn't matter
anymore to keep it a secret. The secret was over.

"That's too bad," my father said. "But it's not
Gloria's fault."

"She found the bottle," I said. "She must be
laughing at me for trying such a stupid idea."

"It's not a stupid idea," my father said.
"You just had bad luck. You know what your

problem is? It's the curve
in the river. Your bottle got
stuck on that curve, and it didn't
have a chance."

I felt a little better. I went to
see Gloria.

"I wanted to give you your bottle back," Gloria
said. Then she added, "I thought it was a great
idea, sending a message in a bottle."

"Well, it's a good idea, but it's a no-good idea
because of the curve in the river. The bottle
couldn't get around it," I explained.

"I guess it couldn't," Gloria said.

"Julian," my father said, "I have to make a
long trip in the truck Saturday. I have to pick up
some car parts. I'm going to go past the big bridge
down the river. Would you like to ride along?"

I said I would.

"You know," my father said, "there's something we could do. We could walk out on the bridge. And if you wanted, you could send a new message. Your bottle would have a good chance from there. It's past the curve in the river."

I thought about it. I decided to do it. And I told my father.

"You know," he said, "if you don't mind my advice—put something special about yourself in the bottle, for the person who finds it."

"Why?" I asked.

"It'll give the wind and the water something special to carry. If you send something you care about, it might bring you luck."

I was working on my new message. And then I thought about Huey and Gloria. I thought how they might want to send bottles too. It didn't seem so important anymore that I be the only one to do it.

And that's what we did. We all got new bottles, and we put something special in each one. We each made a picture of ourselves for our bottle.

And in his, Huey put his favorite joke:
Where does a hamburger go on New Year's Eve?
To a meat ball.

In hers, Gloria put instructions on doing a cartwheel.

In mine, I wrote instructions for taking care of rabbits.

We added our addresses and phone numbers and pushed in the corks tightly. We were ready for Saturday.

The bridge was long and silver and sparkled in the sun. It was so big that it looked like giants must have made it, that human beings never could have. But human beings did.

My father parked below the bridge. "From here we have to walk," he said.

We got out of the truck, which always smells a little bit of dust, but mostly of the raisins Dad keeps on the dashboard.

We walked in the outside walkers' lane to the middle of the river. Cars whizzed past. We each had our bottle in a backpack.

The bridge swayed a little. We could feel it vibrate. My father held Gloria's and Huey's hands. I held Gloria's other hand.

"It's scary, but it's safe," my father said.

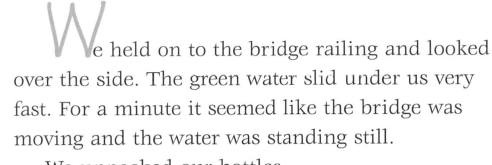

We held on to the bridge railing and looked over the side. The green water slid under us very fast. For a minute it seemed like the bridge was moving and the water was standing still.

We unpacked our bottles.

"Don't just throw them over the side," my father said. "Make some wishes. Sending messages around the world is a big thing to do.

Anytime you do a big thing, it's good to make wishes."

We did.

I don't know what Huey or Gloria wished. I wished our bottles would sail along together. I wished they wouldn't get trapped in seaweed or ice, or hit rocks. I wished we'd make new friends on the other side of the world. I wished we'd go to meet them someday.

"Ready?" my father said.

Together we threw our bottles over the side. They made a tiny splash. They looked very small, but we could see them starting toward the ocean.

They were like Columbus's ships. I hoped they'd stay together a long, long time.

Meet
Ann Cameron

"A book is like a message in a bottle that an author throws out to sea: you never know whom it might reach, or how much it might mean to them."

The idea for stories about Julian, his little brother Huey, and his best friend Gloria came from stories a friend named Julian told Ms. Cameron about his childhood.

Ann Cameron tells of how much she loved watching her grandfather heat bars of iron in his forge. The heavy bars of iron turned red hot and then white hot over the coals. Sparks flew as he hammered them into beautiful and useful things.

"Sometimes I feel like him as my mind hammers at the cold, stiff material of words," Ms. Cameron writes.

Meet
Ann Strugnell

Ann Strugnell has illustrated *The Stories Julian Tells; More Stories Julian Tells;* and *Julian, Dream Doctor.*

Ms. Strugnell studied sculpture before beginning to illustrate children's books. She lives in London, England, with her husband and two sons.

River Winding

Rain falling, what things do you grow?
Snow melting, where do you go?
Wind blowing, what trees do you know?
River winding, where do you flow?

Charlotte Zolotow

The Tide in the River

The tide in the river,
The tide in the river,
The tide in the river runs deep,
I saw a shiver
Pass over the river
As the tide turned in its sleep.

Eleanor Farjeon

READING RESOURCES

CONTENTS

50 ft. (width may vary)

Backboard

Basket

16 ft.

12 ft.

Center circle

Free throw lane (NBA)

BASKET (side view)

10 ft.

REMEMBERING

...eone you ...wing of the ...can deco ...es.

1.

2. Fo

3. Unfo ...t o ...pa

4. Glue the ...or drawing ...part under t ...part you cut

Fold down the t paper. Glue the Then decorate you

col...
scissors
glue
crayons
decor...

CHARTS AND TABLES

SOME DIFFERENT KINDS OF PENGUINS

Name	Where Found	Habitat	Height	Usual Number of Eggs
Emperor Penguin	Antarctica	ocean and pack ice	48 inches (122 cm)	1
Chinstrap Penguin	Antarctica and polar islands	coastal waters	30 inches (75 cm)	2
Adélie Penguin	Antarctica and polar islands	coastal waters	30 inches (75 cm)	2
Snares Island Penguin	New Zealand	coastal waters	29 inches (73 cm)	2
Galápagos Penguin	Galápagos Islands	coastal waters	20 inches (50 cm)	2
Little Penguin	Australia, New Zealand, and nearby islands	coastal waters	16 inches (40 cm)	2

CHARTS AND TABLES

How Far Down the River?

Miles Between River Towns	Red Wing	Point Douglas	Hastings	St. Paul	Minneapolis
Red Wing	—	22	23	48	62
Point Douglas	22	—	1	27	41
Hastings	23	1	—	25	39
St. Paul	48	27	25	—	14
Minneapolis	62	41	39	14	—

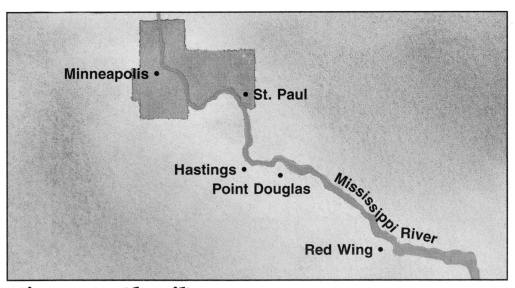

Minnesota (detail)

DIAGRAMS

A Basketball Court

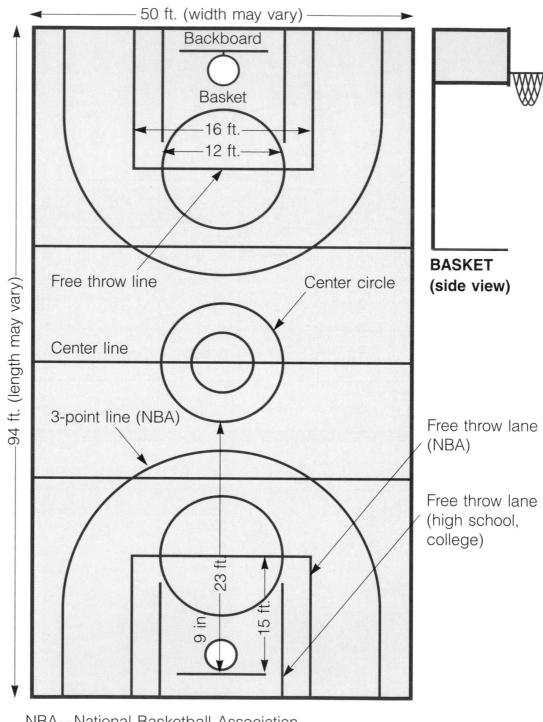

50 ft. (width may vary)

Backboard

Basket

16 ft.

12 ft.

Free throw line

Center circle

Center line

3-point line (NBA)

94 ft. (length may vary)

23 ft.

9 in

15 ft.

BASKET
(side view)

10 ft.

Free throw lane
(NBA)

Free throw lane
(high school,
college)

NBA—National Basketball Association

DIAGRAMS
How a Flood Forms

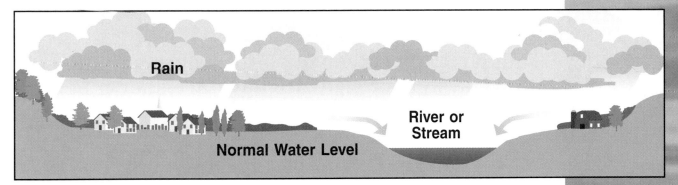

1. Land Stage Water from rain or melted snow falls to the land. After a while, the soil cannot hold any more water. The water begins to move over the land.

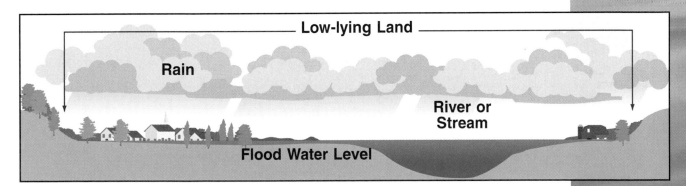

2. Channel Stage The water from rain or melted snow flows into a stream or river. The water begins to rise. Water spills onto the land near the river.

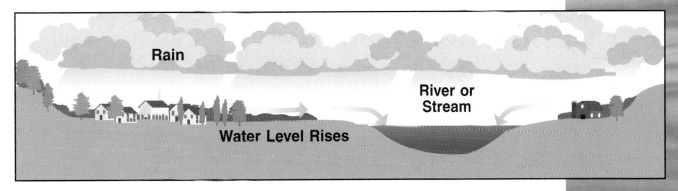

3. Flood Stage Water spills over the banks of a stream or river. The water then spreads across the low-lying land near a stream or river.

DIRECTIONS

SIGN LANGUAGE

The hand signals for the letters of the alphabet in one system of sign language are shown below. When using these signals to "talk" with someone, remember to:

1. Keep your hand where the person you are "talking" to can see it.

2. Make your signals clear and precise.

3. Mark breaks between words by snapping the fingers or by quickly putting both hands together, separating them, and jerking them downward.

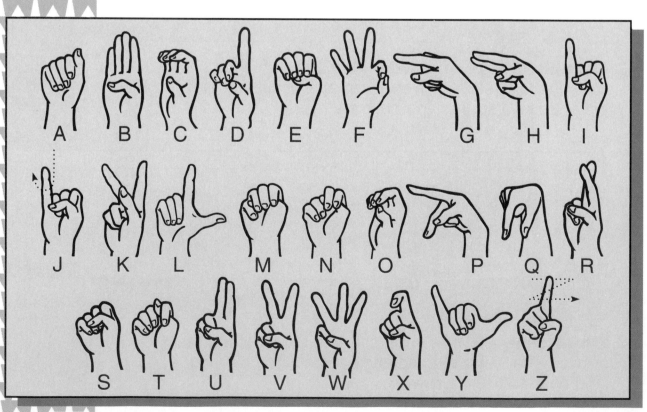

DIRECTIONS

REMEMBERING SOMEONE SPECIAL

Think of someone you like very much. Find a photo or make a drawing of that person. Then make a frame for the picture. You can decorate the frame with things your special person likes.

You will need:

- photo or drawing of a special person
- construction paper
- scissors
- glue
- crayons
- decorations such as cut paper, beads, glitter, yarn, stickers

1. Fold the paper as shown.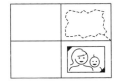

2. Fold again.

3. Unfold the paper. Cut out a wavy frame line in one part.

4. Glue the photo or drawing to the part under the part you cut out.

5. Fold down the top half of the paper. Glue the paper in place. Then decorate your frame.

DIRECTIONS

PLAY NUMBER SPUD

Before Playing: Get a big, soft ball.
Count off so that everyone has a number.

1. One player throws the ball in the air and calls out a number. The others run away.

2. The player whose number was called catches the ball and yells "Freeze!"

3. The player with the ball throws it at the feet of any player close by.

4. The player whose feet are hit calls out **S** for the first letter in **SPUD**. The player then throws the ball in the air, calling out a new number.

5. Each time a player's feet are hit, he or she calls out the next letter of the word **SPUD**. When a player is hit four times and has spelled out **SPUD**, he or she is out.

The way-to-win choices:

- The last two remaining players can be the winners.
- Any player who lasts for ten minutes or more is a winner.
- Invent your own ideas for winning.

FORMS AND APPLICATIONS

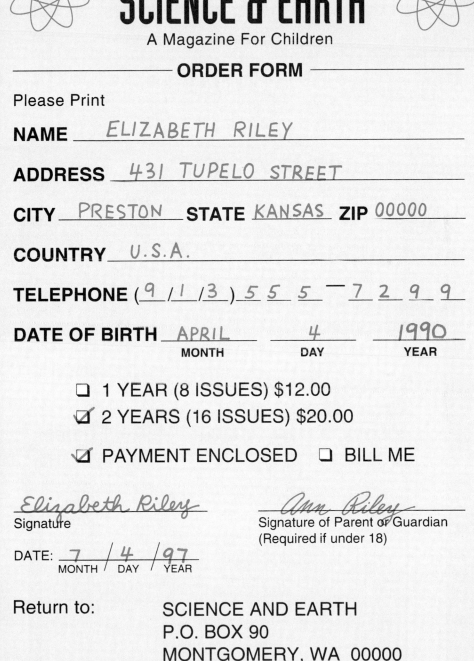

Fun • Informative • Creative

SCIENCE & EARTH

A Magazine For Children

ORDER FORM

Please Print

NAME _ELIZABETH RILEY_

ADDRESS _431 TUPELO STREET_

CITY _PRESTON_ **STATE** _KANSAS_ **ZIP** _00000_

COUNTRY _U.S.A._

TELEPHONE (_9_/_1_/_3_) _5_ _5_ _5_ — _7_ _2_ _9_ _9_

DATE OF BIRTH _APRIL_ _4_ _1990_
                    MONTH   DAY   YEAR

- ❑ 1 YEAR (8 ISSUES) $12.00
- ☑ 2 YEARS (16 ISSUES) $20.00

☑ PAYMENT ENCLOSED ❑ BILL ME

Elizabeth Riley
Signature

Ann Riley
Signature of Parent or Guardian
(Required if under 18)

DATE: _7_/_4_/_97_
      MONTH / DAY / YEAR

Return to: SCIENCE AND EARTH
              P.O. BOX 90
              MONTGOMERY, WA 00000

GRAPHS

Soccer Goals Scored This Season

Player	⚽ = 1 Goal
Abby	⚽⚽⚽⚽⚽⚽⚽⚽⚽⚽
Eric	⚽⚽⚽⚽
Joan	⚽⚽⚽⚽⚽⚽
Jonathan	⚽⚽⚽
Moira	⚽⚽⚽⚽⚽⚽⚽⚽
Toby	⚽⚽⚽⚽⚽⚽⚽

Games Our School Won This Year

☐ = 1 Game

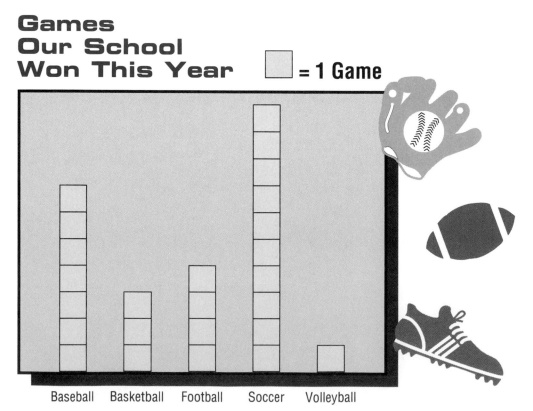

Baseball Basketball Football Soccer Volleyball

MAPS

WEATHER MAP: UNITED STATES

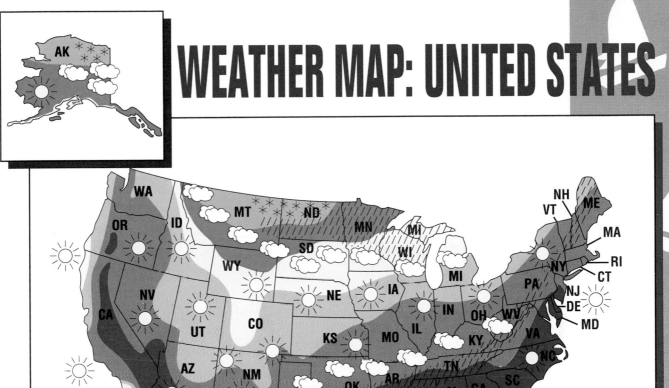

September 17

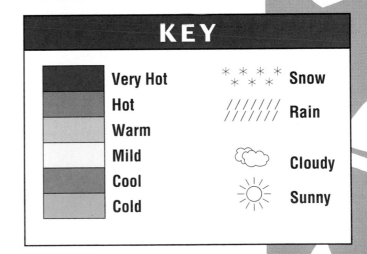

KEY

Very Hot	✳✳✳✳ **Snow**
Hot	⁄⁄⁄⁄⁄⁄⁄ **Rain**
Warm	
Mild	☁ **Cloudy**
Cool	☀ **Sunny**
Cold	

MAPS

Long Meadow Park

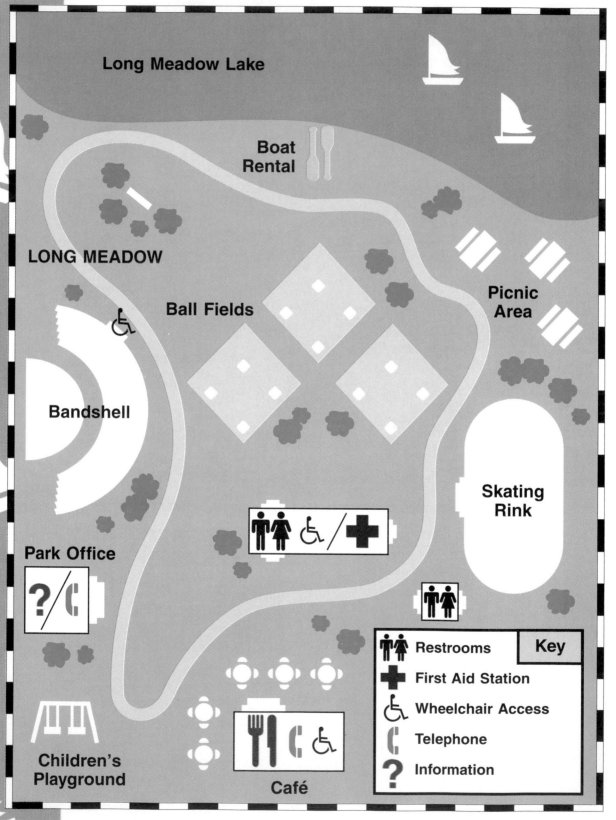

Long Meadow Lake

Boat Rental

LONG MEADOW

Ball Fields

Picnic Area

Bandshell

Skating Rink

Park Office

Children's Playground

Café

Key

👫 Restrooms

✚ First Aid Station

♿ Wheelchair Access

☎ Telephone

? Information

MAPS

SOUTH AMERICA
INCA LANDS
KEY
- Inca lands
- ----- Modern boundary
- (Peru) Modern country

(Colombia)
(Ecuador)
SOUTH
AMERICA
(Peru)
(Bolivia)
ATLANTIC
OCEAN
PACIFIC
OCEAN
(Chile)
(Argentina)

N
W—E
S

COLOMBIA
⊛ Quito
ECUADOR
Putumayo
Amazon
Ucayali
Javari
BRAZIL
PERU
Lima ⊛
Lake Titicaca
BOLIVIA
La Paz ⊛
Lake Poopó
CHILE
A N D E S   M O U N T A I N S

PACIFIC
OCEAN

N
W—E
S

PERU: Landforms
KEY
- Mountains   ⊛ National capital
- Hills   —— National boundary
- Plains   〜 River

GLOS

This glossary can help you
to find out the meanings of
words in this book that you may
not know.

SARY

The words are listed in alphabetical order. Guide words at the top of each page tell you the first and last words on the page.

Aa

allowance

An **allowance** is an amount of money that is given to someone. Kevin gets an allowance once a week. ▲ **allowances.**

ancient

When something is **ancient,** it is very old. Leslie wants to visit the **ancient** pyramids in Egypt during her vacation.

ancient

arrow

1. A symbol shaped like an **arrow,** that points the way to something. The **arrow** on the sign shows the way to the beach.
2. An **arrow** is a thin stick that has a point at one end and feathers at the other. An **arrow** can be shot from a bow. ▲ **arrows.**

Bb

beach

A **beach** is a rocky or sandy strip of land that is close to a lake or an ocean. The **beach** is covered with sand.
▲ **beaches.**

bottle

A **bottle** is something that is used to hold liquids. A **bottle** may be made of glass or plastic. ▲ **bottles.**

bought

Bought comes from the word **buy**. I **bought** Pam a book for her birthday.

bounce

Bounce means to move back after hitting something. Cal threw the ball and watched it **bounce** off the sidewalk. ▲ **bounced, bouncing.**

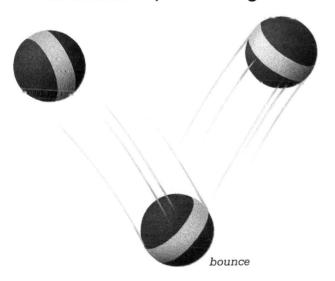

bounce

brace

A **brace** is something that holds parts together or keeps a thing from shaking. Andy wore a metal **brace** on his leg to help him walk. ▲ **braces.**

brave

If you are **brave**, it means that you are not afraid. The **brave** man climbed up the tall tree to get the kitten down safely. ▲ **braver, bravest.**

break

When something **breaks**, it divides into pieces. If you drop that mirror on the floor, it will **break.** ▲ **broke, broken, breaking.**

breeze

A **breeze** is a soft, gentle wind. The ocean **breeze** made us feel cool. ▲ **breezes.**

buy

When you **buy** something, it means you pay money for it. My grandmother sent us to the supermarket to **buy** orange juice. ▲ **bought, buying.**

G3

Cc

chance

Chance means that something might happen. There is a **chance** that it may snow tomorrow. ▲ **chances.**

charge

Charge means to rush at something. The angry bull started to **charge** the farmer.

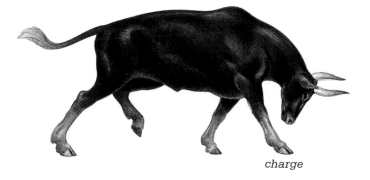
charge

chase

Chase means to run after something and try to catch it. My dog likes to **chase** the car down the road. ▲ **chased, chasing.**

club

A **club** is a group of people who meet together for fun or some special purpose. Our book **club** will meet next Friday. ▲ **clubs.**

cover

To **cover** means to put something over or on something else. **Cover** the baby with a blanket so she won't get cold. ▲ **covered, covering.**

crawl

Crawl means to move slowly on your hands and knees. The baby is just beginning to learn how to **crawl.** ▲ **crawled, crawling.**

creek

A **creek** is a small stream. Josie's father taught her how to fish in a **creek.** ▲ **creeks.**

Dd

danger

Danger is anything that could cause harm or injury to you. The fire alarm sounded to warn people of the **danger**. ▲ **dangers.**

driver

A person who controls and steers a car, train, truck, or bus is a **driver.** The bus **driver** turned left onto Elm Street. ▲ **drivers.**

driver

during

During means at the same time as something else. Please try not to talk **during** the concert.

Ee

edge

An **edge** is the line or place where something ends. The dime rolled off the **edge** of the table. ▲ **edges.**

enemy

An **enemy** is a person, or group of people, who hates someone else. The cruel king was the **enemy** of his subjects. ▲ **enemies.**

enough

Enough means that there is as much of something as you need. There was **enough** food for everyone.

except

Except means that something or someone has not been included. Everyone **except** Joe was at the party.

expect

Expect means to think that something will happen. We **expect** fifty people to come to the family picnic on Sunday. ▲ **expected, expecting.**

Ff

fair

A **fair** is a place where people show and sell things they have grown or made. Benito won first prize for his pet pig at the state **fair.** ▲ **fairs.**

field

A **field** is an area of land where some games are played. Football is played on a **field.** ▲ **fields.**

float

To **float** means to rest on top of water or other liquid. We watched the leaf **float** down the stream. ▲ **floated, floating.**

float

flood

Flood means to cover with water. Did Jim **flood** the kitchen floor with water when he did the dishes? ▲ **flooded, flooding.**

footprint

A **footprint** is a mark made by a foot or shoe. We could see a **footprint** in the wet sand.

▲ **footprints.**

fountain

A **fountain** is a stream of water that shoots up into the air. José drank from the water **fountain.**

▲ **fountains.**

fountain

frighten

Frighten means to make a person or an animal afraid or scared. The cat tried to **frighten** the birds away.

▲ **frightened, frightening.**

Gg

gather

Gather means to collect or bring things or people together. We will all **gather** in the park tomorrow night to watch the fireworks.

▲ **gathered, gathering.**

Hh

hope

Hope means to want something very much. We **hope** that tomorrow will be a warm and sunny day so we can have a picnic at the beach.

▲ **hoped, hoping.**

horn

A **horn** is something you push, squeeze, or blow to make a sound. Ben squeezed the **horn** on his bicycle so everyone would know he was coming.
▲ **horns.**

howl

To **howl** means to make a loud wailing cry. The wind **howls** through the old house during a storm.
▲ **howled, howling.**

huge

Huge means very, very big. An elephant is a **huge** animal.

huge

Kk

kinfolk

Kinfolk are a person's relatives or family. All of my **kinfolk** live in the same city.

Ll

language

The words we speak, read, and write are called **language.** The second **language** Bridgette learned was Spanish.
▲ **languages.**

listen

Listen means to try to hear in a careful way. The children liked to **listen** to the story. ▲ **listened, listening.**

lock

A **lock** is a special part of a waterway or canal that ships use to go from one body of water to another. The ship was in the **lock,** waiting to enter the bay. ▲ **locks.**

Mm

meadow

A **meadow** is a field of grassy land. A **meadow** is often used for growing hay or as a pasture for animals. ▲ **meadows.**

member

When you belong to a group, you are a **member** of it. Even though it is a very large animal, the lion is a **member** of the cat family. ▲ **members.**

message

A **message** is information sent from one person to another. Mom called and left a **message** that she would be late. ▲ **messages.**

mountain

1. A large pile of things can be called a mountain. We had a **mountain** of laundry to wash on Saturday.

2. A **mountain** is a very high area of land. The **mountain** was high, and very hard to climb. ▲ **mountains.**

mountain

muddy

When something is **muddy** it is covered in wet dirt. Ken's boots were **muddy** after running through the woods. ▲ **muddier, muddiest.**

Nn

neighbor

A **neighbor** is someone who lives near you. Our **neighbor** cared for our dog when we went on vacation. ▲ **neighbors.**

Pp

pass

Pass means to move something from one person to another. Please **pass** the cereal to me. ▲ **passed, passing.**

peek

Peek means to look at something quickly or without anyone knowing. The squirrels **peek** out from behind the tree. ▲ **peeked, peeking.**

perfect

When something is **perfect,** it means that nothing is wrong with it. Jane's math test was **perfect.**

piano

A **piano** is a large musical instrument that has black and white keys. Ian practices the **piano** every day. ▲ **pianos.**

piano

pile

A **pile** is a lot of things lying on top of each other. We put all our old newspapers and magazines in a **pile** by the door. ▲ **piles.**

plain

A **plain** is an area of flat or almost flat land. As we drove across the **plain** we could see for miles. ▲ **plains.**

pocket

A **pocket** is a place to hold things that is sewn into clothing, bags, or suitcases. Barbara put her gloves in one **pocket** and her keys in another **pocket. ▲ pockets.**

point

Point means a certain moment in time. Jerry reached the **point** where he was so tired that he fell asleep. ▲ **points.**

porch

A **porch** is a part of a house that is outdoors. We sit on our **porch** in the summer because it is cool there. ▲ **porches.**

porch

prize

A **prize** is something that is won for doing very well in a contest or game. Janice's painting won first **prize** at the art show. ▲ **prizes.**

promise

To **promise** means to say that you will be sure to do something. Lionel made a **promise** not to tell my secret to anyone. ▲ **promised, promising.**

Qq

quit

Quit means to stop doing something. Joe **quit** swimming when he got cold. ▲ **quit, quitting.**

Rr

radio

A **radio** is a machine that you can turn on to listen to music, news, or other programs. Some evenings we listen to music on our **radio.** ▲ **radios.**

rage

Rage means to act or move with great force or violence. The weatherman watched the storm **rage** along the coast. ▲ **raged, raging.**

repair

Repair means to fix or mend something in order to put it into good condition again. Will she **repair** the broken leg of the table today?
▲ **repaired, repairing.**

repair

river

A **river** is water that is always moving from high ground to low ground. A **river** ends when it comes to another **river,** a lake, a sea, or an ocean. ▲ **rivers.**

rough

1. Something that is **rough** feels full of bumps. The bark of a tree feels **rough**.
2. **Rough** also means not gentle. The ocean was **rough** during the terrible storm. ▲ **rougher, roughest.**

rule

A **rule** tells you what you can do and what you cannot do. One **rule** at school is that you cannot run in the hallways. ▲ **rules.**

Ss

sail

Sail means to move over water. The children liked to **sail** their toy boats on the pond. ▲ **sailed, sailing.**

sand

Sand is a kind of earth that is made of tiny pieces of rock. There is **sand** on beaches and in deserts.

sand

score

1. A **score** is the number of points or the record of points made in a game or on a test. The final **score** was 5 to 4. ▲ **scores.**
2. When you make a point or points in a game or test, you **score** points. Rick **scored** two goals in the soccer game yesterday. ▲ **scored, scoring.**

serious

When you are **serious**, you are not silly or joking. The doctor was **serious** when he spoke to my mom

ship

A **ship** is a large boat that travels across deep water. There is a **ship** in the harbor. ▲ **ships.**

ship

shoulder

Your **shoulder** is the top part of your arm where it joins your body. I ripped my sweater at the shoulder. ▲ **shoulders.**

sidewalk

A **sidewalk** is a path to walk on next to the street. I walked home on the **sidewalk.** ▲ **sidewalks**

slide

Slide means to move easily on something. Please **slide** the book across the table to me. ▲ **slid, sliding.**

smooth

If something is **smooth**, you do not feel any bumps on it when you touch it. The skin of the apple is very **smooth.** ▲ **smoother, smoothest.**

sneak

Sneak means to move or act in a secret or sly way. The children tried to **sneak** into the theater. ▲ **sneaked** or **snuck, sneaking.**

softly

When something is done **softly,** it is done in a quiet or gentle way. Mother spoke **softly** because my sister was sleeping. ▲ **softer, softest.**

solid

When something is **solid,** it is hard and has a shape. When we freeze water, it becomes **solid.**

splash

Splash means to throw water or some other liquid around. Stand back or the car will **splash** you.
▲ **splashed, splashing.**

stout

Stout means thick and heavy. The baseball player was strong and **stout.**
▲ **stouter, stoutest**

stranger

A **stranger** is a person you do not know. A **stranger** rang our doorbell. ▲ **strangers.**

stream

A **stream** is water that is moving. Everyone stared at the fish splashing in the **stream.** ▲ **streams.**

stretch

When you **stretch** something, you make it as long as it can be. I like to **stretch** my arms when I wake up in the morning.
▲ **stretched, stretching**

stretch

suppose

If you **suppose** something will happen, it means that you think it will happen. I **suppose** it will rain this afternoon. ▲ **supposed, supposing.**

sweet

If a person or thing is **sweet,** it means they are kindly or pleasant. My grandmother is **sweet.** ▲ **sweeter, sweetest.**

swing

When you **swing** something, you make it move back and forth through the air. Patricia likes to **swing** her arms when she walks.

▲ **swung, swinging.**

Tt

team

A **team** is a group of people who play a game together. There are twenty people on our school's football **team.**

▲ **teams**

thin

Thin means not fat. A horse has a long, **thin** face. ▲ **thinner, thinnest.**

throne

A **throne** is a big chair that a king or queen sits on during special occasions. The day the princess became queen, she sat on her **throne** for the first time. ▲ **thrones.**

throne

tide

Tide means the regular rise and fall of the water in the oceans caused by the pull of the sun and moon on the earth. High **tide** happens twice a day. ▲ **tides.**

tie

When a game ends in a **tie,** it means that both teams have the same score, so neither team wins or loses. The soccer team came back to **tie** the game. ▲ **ties, tied.**

touch

Touch means to put your hand on something. Don't **touch** the hot stove. ▲ **touched, touching.**

travel

Travel means to go from one place to another. We will **travel** by car. ▲ **traveled, traveling.**

Uu

understand

When you **understand** something, you know what it means. Andy can **understand** both English and Spanish. ▲ **understood, understanding.**

Vv

valley

A **valley** is the low land between hills or mountains. The **valley** has a river flowing through it. ▲ **valleys.**

valley

village

A **village** is a small group of houses. A **village** is usually smaller than a town. We drove through a tiny **village** in the mountains. ▲ **villages.**

village

Ww

warn

When someone tells you ahead of time to watch out for something that may happen. Did you **warn** him that it might rain? ▲ **warned, warning.**

whisper

Whisper means to speak in a very quiet voice. The teacher asked the students to **whisper** when they shared their stories. ▲ **whispered, whispering.**

whistle

1. A **whistle** is something you blow into that makes a sound. The police officer blew a **whistle** and all the cars stopped. ▲ **whistles.**
2. When you **whistle**, you make a sound by pushing air out though your lips or teeth. My dog always comes when I **whistle.** ▲ **whistled, whistling.**

whole

When something is **whole**, it has no parts missing from it. Twelve eggs make up a **whole** dozen.

ACKNOWLEDGMENTS

The publisher gratefully acknowledges permission to reprint the following copyrighted material:

"And Then" by Prince Redcloud. Used by permission of Lee Bennett Hopkins for the author. All rights reserved.

"Angel Child, Dragon Child" from ANGEL CHILD, DRAGON CHILD with text by Michele Maria Surat and pictures by Vo-Dinh-Mai. Text copyright © 1983 by Carnival Press, Inc. Illustrations copyright © 1983 by Vo-Dinh Mai. Permission to reprint the art from Vo-Dinh-Mai. Published by arrangement with Raintree/Steck-Vaughn Publishers. All rights reserved.

"April Rain Song" from THE DREAM KEEPER by Langston Hughes. Copyright © 1932 by Alfred A. Knopf, Inc. and renewed 1960 by Langston Hughes. Reprinted by permission of the publisher.

"The Best Friends Club." This is the entire text and nineteen illustrations from THE BEST FRIENDS CLUB by Elizabeth Winthrop with illustrations by Martha Weston. Text copyright © 1989 by Elizabeth Winthrop. Illustrations copyright © 1989 by Martha Weston. Reprinted by permission of William Morrow and Company, Inc./Publishers, New York.

Text and art of "Best Wishes, Ed" from WINSTON, NEWTON, ELTON, AND ED by James Stevenson. Copyright © 1978 by James Stevenson. Reprinted by permission of Greenwillow Books, a division of William Morrow and Company, Inc.

"Colores de Caracol" ("The rainbow showing") from VERY VERY SHORT NATURE POEMS by Ernesto Galarza. Copyright © 1972 by Ernesto Galarza. Reprinted by permission of Mrs. Mae Galarza.

"Come a Tide" from COME A TIDE by George Ella Lyon, pictures by Stephen Gammell. Text Copyright © 1990 by George Ella Lyon. Illustrations © 1990 by Stephen Gammell. All rights reserved. Reprinted by Permission of Orchard Books, New York.

"A Curve in the River" from MORE STORIES JULIAN TELLS by Ann Cameron. Illustrated by Ann Strugnell. Text copyright © 1986 by Ann Strugnell. Reprinted by permission of HarperCollins Publishers.

"Dear Daddy ..." from DEAR DADDY by Philippe Dupasquier. Copyright © 1985 by Philippe Dupasquier. Reprinted with the permission of Simon & Schuster Books For Young Readers.

"Eletelephony" from TIRRA LIRRA: RHYMES OLD AND NEW by Laura E. Richards. Copyright 1930, 1932 by Laura E. Richards. Copyright © renewed 1960 by Hamilton Richards. By permission Little, Brown and Company.

"Finding a Way" by Myra Cohn Livingston reprinted with permission of Margaret K. McElderry Books, an imprint of Simon & Schuster Children's Publishing Division, from THERE WAS A PLACE AND OTHER POEMS by Myra Cohn Livingston. Copyright © 1988 by Myra Cohn Livingston.

"Ham Radio" by Kenny A. Chaffin, from U. S. KIDS, Vol. 5, No. 2, February 1992 issue. Copyright © 1992, by Children's Better Health Institute, Benjamin Franklin Literary and Medical Society, Incorporated. Reprinted by permission.

Cover illustration from IT COULD BE WORSE! by James Stevenson. Copyright (c) 1977 by James Stevenson. By permission of Greenwillow Books, a division of William Morrow and Company, Inc.

"It's Dark in Here" from WHERE THE SIDEWALK ENDS by Shel Silverstein. Copyright © 1974 by Evil Eye Music, Inc. Reprinted by permission of HarperCollins Publishers.

Cover, JAMAICA AND BRIANNA by Juanita Havill. Jacket art copyright (c) 1993 by Anne Sibley O'Brien. Reprinted by permission of Houghton Mifflin Company. All rights reserved.

JAMAICA TAG-ALONG. Text copyright (c) 1989 by Juanita Havill. Illustrations copyright by Anne Sibley O'Brien. Reprinted by permission of Houghton Mifflin Company. All rights reserved.

Cover, JAMAICA'S FIND by Juanita Havill. Jacket art copyright (c) 1986 by Anne Sibley O'Brien. Reprinted by permission of Houghton Mifflin Company. All rights reserved.

"Laura" from THE BUTTERFLY JAR by Jeff Moss. Copyright © 1989 by Jeff Moss. Used by permission of Bantam Books, a division of Bantam Doubleday Dell Publishing Group, Inc.

Cover illustration from LIZZIE AND HAROLD by Elizabeth Winthrop. Illustrated by Martha Weston. Illustration copyright (c) 1986 by Martha Weston. By permission of Lothrop, Lee & Shepard Books, a division of William Morrow and Company, Inc.

"Llama and the Great Flood." This is the entire work from LLAMA AND THE GREAT FLOOD: A FOLKTALE FROM PERU by Ellen Alexander. Copyright © 1989 by Ellen Alexander. Reprinted by permission of HarperCollins Publishers.

"Our Soccer League" from OUR SOCCER LEAGUE by Chuck Solomon. Copyright © 1988 by Chuck Solomon. Reprinted by permission of Crown Publishers.

"Postcards from the Earth" Copyright 1992 Children's Television Workshop (New York, New York). All rights reserved.

"Princess Pooh" is the entire text from PRINCESS POOH by Kathleen M. Muldoon with illustrations by Linda Shute. Text copyright © 1989 by Kathleen M. Muldoon. Illustrations copyright © 1989 by Linda Shute. Originally published in hardcover by Albert Whitman & Company. All rights reserved. Used with permission.

Entire text, art, and cover of PUFF...FLASH...BANG! by Gail Gibbons. Copyright (c) 1993 by Gail Gibbons. By permission of Morrow Junior Books, a division of William Morrow and Company, Inc.

"River Winding" is the text of RIVER WINDING by Charlotte Zolotow. Copyright © 1970 by Charlotte Zolotow. Reprinted by permission of HarperCollins Publishers.

"Since Hanna Moved Away" by Judith Viorst. Reprinted with permission of Atheneum Books for Young Readers, an imprint of Simon & Schuster Children's Publishing Division, from IF I WERE IN CHARGE OF THE WORLD AND OTHER WORRIES by Judith Viorst. Copyright © 1981 by Judith Viorst.

Cover illustration from SONG AND DANCE MAN by Karen Ackerman. Illustrated by Stephen Gammell. Illustration copyright © 1988 by Stephen Gammell. Reprinted by permission of Alfred A. Knopf.

Cover illustration from THE STORIES JULIAN TELLS by Ann Cameron. Illustrated by Ann Strugnell. Illustrations copyright © 1981 by Ann Strugnell. Reprinted by permission of Pantheon Books, a division of Random House, Inc.

"The Sun, the Wind and the Rain" from THE SUN, THE WIND AND THE RAIN by Lisa Westberg Peters. Text copyright © 1988 by Lisa Westberg Peters. Illustration copyright © 1988 by Ted Rand. Reprinted by permission of Henry Holt and Co., Inc.

"Tagalongs" from U. S. KIDS, Vol. 2, No. 5, April 1989 issue. Copyright © 1989 by Field Publications. Reprinted by permission.

"There Was An Old Pig With a Pen" is the text and art for this selection from THE BOOK OF PIGERICKS; PIG LIMERICKS by Arnold Lobel. Copyright © 1983 by Arnold Lobel. Reprinted by permission of HarperCollins Publishers.

"The Tide in the River" by Eleanor Farjeon reprinted by permission of Harold Ober Associates, Incorporated. Copyright © 1920 by Eleanor Farjeon. Renewed 1948.

"True But Strange" Copyright 1994 Children's Television Network (New York, New York). All rights reserved.

"An umbrella and a raincoat" by Buson. Reprinted with permission of Simon & Schuster Books for Young Readers, an imprint of Simon & Schuster Children's Publishing Division, from DON'T TELL THE SCARECROW AND OTHER JAPANESE POEMS by Issa, et al. Copyright © 1969.

"Until I Saw the Sea" from I FEEL THE SAME WAY by Lilian Moore. Copyright © 1967 by Lilian Moore. Reprinted by permission of Marian Reiner for the author.

"Water" by Joan Bransfield Graham. Reprinted by permission.

"The Water-Go-Round" by Dennis Lee. Reprinted by permission.

"We're Racing, Racing Down the Walk" by Phyllis McGinley. Reprinted by permission.

Cover illustration from WHAT'S UNDER MY BED? by James Stevenson. Copyright (c) 1983 by James Stevenson. By permission of Greenwillow Books, a division of William Morrow & Company, Inc.

"Write About a Radish" Text from "Write About a Radish" from DOGS & DRAGONS, TREES & DREAMS by Karla Kuskin. This poem originally appeared in NEAR THE WINDOW TREE by Karla Kuskin. Copyright © 1975 by Karla Kuskin. Reprinted by permission of HarperCollins Publishers.

COVER DESIGN: Carbone Smolan Associates
COVER ILLUSTRATION: Daniel Kirk (front - winged letter), Etienne Delessert (front - birds), Lambert Davis (back)

DESIGN CREDITS
Carbone Smolan Associates, front matter and unit openers
Bill Smith Studio, 34-35, 94-97, 148-149, 200-201, 312-315
Function Thru Form, Inc., 334-335, 337-339, 341-342, 346
Sheldon Cotler + Associates Editorial Group, 230- 257, 260-289, 292-311, 318-333
Notovitz Design Inc., 336, 340, 343-345, 347

ILLUSTRATION CREDITS
Unit 1: Daniel Kirk, 10-11; Mark Kaplan, 12; Emily Thompson, 34-35; John Kane, 38-39; Cheryl Arnemann, 66-67; Chris Spollen, 94, 96-97; Kelly Hume, 98-121. **Unit 2:** Etienne Delessert, 124-125; Gary Torrisi, 126-147 (bkgds.); Jerry Dadds, 261; Bob Wright Creative Group, 152-153; Frank McSane 172-173; Judy Love, 174-175; Denise Brunkus, 226-227. **Unit 3:** Lambert Davis, 228-229; David Goldin, 230, 256-257; Andy Levine, 261; Sandra Speidel, 262-287; Sally Vitsky, 290-291; S C & A, 292-311. **Reading Resources:** Alex Bloch, 336; Patrick O'Brien, 337; Maria Lauricella, 338, 346; Graphic Chart and Map Co., 347; Bob Mansfield, 339; Felicia Telsey, 341; Nelle Davis, 342. **Glossary:** Will and Cory Nelson, G3, G4, G8; Bob Pepper, G7, G12, G15.

The Test-Taker's HANDBOOK

How to Use This Handbook

Sometimes, taking a test can make you a little upset. These pages will help you feel better about taking tests.

You will find information and hints to help with different kinds of questions. You will also learn how to use what you know to make taking tests a little easier. Try to take notes or make up rhymes or other games to help you remember the information.

This section will help with all kinds of tests. It will help with tests that your teacher gives you. It will also help you with special tests that you might have to take.

Before you take a test, try to look at this section again. Each time you read it, you will remember more about taking tests. That will help you be a better test-taker.

Hints for Taking Tests

Do you think that Sammy Sosa practices before a big baseball game? Sure he does!

Before you take a test, you can practice, too.

Think about these hints and strategies. Practice as many of these as you can.

It Takes Practice

Practice to get in shape before a test.

FIND OUT

★ Ask your teacher what will be on the test.

★ Will it be a book test?

★ Will it be a special test, such as the SAT?

LOOK BACK

★ Check old tests. Look at old practice papers.

★ Review what you did right.

★ Make sure you understand what you did wrong.

Do not **disturb**.

○ hurt

○ tell

○ bother

○ walk

What came first in the passage?

○ The puppy found the spider.

○ The boy looked for his puppy.

○ The puppy got out of the yard.

○ The spider scared the puppy.

What is the main idea of the poem?

○ Rain soaks the grass.

○ We need all kinds of weather.

○ Windy days are fun.

○ The sun is warm.

Show What You Know

Do you get a little nervous when you have to take a test? That's OK — it happens to many of us.

Take a deep breath and say, "I am ready. I can do this."

Sometimes it helps to think about work you have done before.

Review reading strategies that you already know.

Oh, I remember doing one like this for homework.

Hmm, I better check this answer again.

TRY:

★ rereading

★ looking for clue words

★ using other words in the sentence

★ thinking about synonyms

Tick, Tick, Tick

Most tests are timed, but time can be on your side. Just play it smart.

- Take some time to study before the test.

- Skip items that you are not sure of. Come back to them later.

- Try to sum up the information. It's faster than rereading.

Double Check

- When you finish an item, ask yourself these questions:

  ☐ Is my answer reasonable?

  ☐ Did I answer the question?

- Try to find the answer in the passage.

Preparing for Tests

A multiple-choice test can be the easiest kind of a test. Why? Because you know that one of the choices is the right answer. All you have to do is figure out which one it is.

O blue crayons
O black pens
O red paint
● green markers

Remember to fill in only one circle for each question.

Completely fill in the correct circle for each item.

Ashley and Theo stood on the platform.

"Mom, when will the train get in?" Ashley asked. "I can't wait to meet Uncle Taylor."

"It's almost here," Mom answered.

"Yes," cried Theo, "I can see the light down the track!"

Find and reread the word in the story.

1 The word <u>platform</u> in this story means
   O something to wear
   O a place to wait for a train
   O a train
   O tracks

Sometimes answers don't make sense. Ignore those choices right away.

2 Who were Ashley and Theo waiting for?
   O Mom
   O Dad
   O Uncle Taylor
   O Uncle Theo

Practicing Reading Tests

Directions

Read the passage. Then read each question about the story. Choose the best answer to each question. Mark the space for the answer you have chosen.

Look for key words to help you find the answer.

To play stoop tag, you need at least three people. Many more can play, though. First, decide who is "It." This person chases the others and tries to tag them. Anyone who gets tagged must stoop down and stay there. When another player taps those who are stooping, they can get up and run again. If the person who is "It" tags everyone and everyone is stooping, then the game is over.

Use other words in the sentence to help you learn the meaning of a new word.

1 Who tags the players as they run?

○ the player who is "It"

○ the last player

○ the players who are stooping

○ everyone

2 What does <u>stoop</u> mean in this passage?

○ tap a player

○ run

○ hide

○ bend down

Practicing Reading Tests

Directions

Read the letter. Then read each question about the letter. Choose the best answer to each question. Mark the space for the answer you have chosen.

Dear Maribel,

Today was the big soccer game at school. I was a bit nervous, but I was excited, too. It was the biggest game I ever played in.

The coach helped us practice before the game. That really helped, because we were playing against a very good team.

Mom, Dad, and Grandpa were cheering us on. Even though we lost, our team played very well. Everyone was proud of us. Maybe you can come to our games next season. I think you would enjoy them.

Your cousin,

Mara

> Try to match words in the passage with words in the question.

> Use special clues to help you find the answer.

3 Who helped the team before the game?

- ○ Grandpa
- ○ Maribel
- ○ the coach
- ○ your cousin

4 Who wrote the letter?

- ○ Dad
- ○ the coach
- ○ Maribel
- ○ Mara